CIRONE'S *LOOMIS*
Pocket Dictionary
of Foreign Musical Terms

FEATURING

- More than 4000 foreign musical terms

- Italian, French and German

- More than 160 musical examples

- Comprehensive sections for percussion
  and strings

COMPILED AND EDITED BY ANTHONY J. CIRONE

D1115849

Published By
MEREDITH MUSIC PUBLICATIONS

a division of G.W. Music, Inc.
4899 Lerch Creek Ct., Galesville, MD 20765

MEREDITH MUSIC PUBLICATIONS and its stylized double **M** logo are trademarks of MEREDITH MUSIC PUBLICATIONS, a division of G.W. Music, Inc.

Cover design: Shawn Girsberger
Text Editor: Josie Cirone
Formatting and Proof Reading: Kris Lou

ISBN - 13: 978-1-57463-124-1
Library of Congress Control Number: 2008908125

Foreword

Orchestral musicians, composers, and conductors live in a world dominated by foreign musical terms. Today, students study Spanish, in preference to Italian, French, and German; but it's interesting that even Spanish composers use Italian when writing! That's why this Dictionary is an essential resource for translation in the orchestral music field.

As opposed to other general music dictionaries, this one is listed by language. It also includes two very special sections — percussion and strings — with specific musical terms not found in other publications.

Tante grazie, merci beaucoup, and *vielen Dank* to my colleagues, listed on the following page, for their time, expertise, and contributions.

AJC

With Special Thanks To:

Virginia Baker
Isabelle Chapuis
Ernestine Chihuaria
John Delevoryas
Laurie McGaw
Diane Nicholeris
Andrea Sauer
Mark Starr

Table of Contents

Tempo Indications – Italian

From Slow to Fast

Larghissimo
Very Slow: *The ending "issimo" is the superlative form of the word, in this case, the slowest form of* Largo. Larghississimo *is even slower.*

Largo
Slow, large, broad, stately: *The slowest tempo marking.*

Larghetto
Slightly faster than Largo: *The ending "etto" is always a diminutive in Italian and means "less." In this case, less slow — therefore faster.*

Adagissimo
Slower than Adagio

Adagio
Slowly, softly, peacefully

Adagietto
Slightly faster than Adagio: *The diminutive, less slow — therefore faster.*

Lentissimo
Slower than Lento

Lento
Slowly, but not dragging: *Faster than* Adagio, *this tempo occurs between* Adagio *and* Andante.

Andante
Moderately slow, easily flowing: *Somewhere between* Lento *and* Moderato, *traditionally described as a "walking tempo."*

Andantino

A bit quicker than Andante: *Again, a diminutive meaning "less than." The problem here is in describing "less Andante" as less fast or less slow. Traditionally we think of* Andantino *as faster than* Andante, *however, some conductors consider this slower than* Andante.

Moderato

At a moderate tempo: *Faster than* Andante. *This tempo occurs between* Andante *and* Allegro.

Allegretto

Not quite as fast as Allegro but with the same character: *In this case, the diminutive ending results in a slower tempo (less fast).*

Allegro

Fast, lively, cheerful

Allegrissimo

Faster than Allegro: *The superlative degree of* Allegro, *but not as fast as* Presto.

Presto

Fast, rapid: *Faster than* Allegro.

Prestissimo

Very fast: *The superlative degree of* Presto, *the fastest tempo.*

Additional Tempo Indications

A tempo
In the time of the preceding tempo: *Depending how this is used, it can mean the tempo immediately preceding or going back to the initial tempo.*

Come prima
As before: *Usually referring to the previous tempo, but sometimes refers to playing in the same manner as before.*

Doppio
Double tempo, twice as fast

L'istesso tempo
The same tempo as before: *This always refers to the immediately preceding tempo.*

Scherzo
Jokingly, humorous: *Technically not a tempo marking; however, composers use it in this manner. The tempos are usually fast, but the "joke" element can be light and playful or serious and sinister as with Mahler.*

Vivace
Brisk, lively, vivacious: *When standing alone as a tempo, it usually exceeds an* Allegro.

Vivacissimo
Extremely fast

Tempo Indications – French

Grave   Slow, serious, grievous: *Similar to "Largo" in Italian.*

Plus Lent que Lent   Slower than Lent

Lent   Slowly: *Similar to "Lento" in Italian.*

Modèré   Moderate: *Similar to "Moderato" in Italian.*

Animé   Fast, lively, animated: *Similar to "Allegro" in Italian.*

Vif   Fast, lively: *Similar to "Presto" in Italian.*

Additional Tempo Indications

Au Mouvt. Initial   Beginning tempo

Rapide   Rapid, quick: *Similar to "Vivace" in Italian.*

Tempo Indications – German

Breit Slow, broad: *Similar to "Largo" in Italian.*

Langsam Slow: *Similar to "Lento" in Italian.*

Mäßig Moderate: *Similar to "Moderato" in Italian.*

Gehend Moderately slow: *From the verb to go or to walk in German. Similar to "Andante" in Italian (in a walking manner). Gehend is rarely found in the literature.*

Lebhaft Lively, animated: *Similar to "Allegro" in Italian.*

Schnell Fast, quickly: *Similar to "Presto" in Italian.*

Additional Tempo Indications

Doppel Double, as in double tempo: *Similar to "Doppio movimento" in Italian.*

Erstes Zeitmass A tempo, Beginning tempo

Musical Directives – Italian

A

ab	From, on
abandonandosi	With abandon
a battuta	With the beat, in strict time
abbassare	Tune down: *For string players, a request to purposely tune down a string for a special effect. See "heraustimmen" on page 229.*
abbellimenti	Ornaments or embellishments: *See "acciaccatura" and "appoggiatura" on pages 12 and 15.*
a cappella	Vocal chorus: *Without accompaniment.*
accalorarsi	To get excited, aroused
accanito	Fierce, tenacious
accarezzevole	Caressingly
accelerando	(*accel.*)Accelerate: *Moving faster.*
accentato	Accented, marked
accènto	Accent:

acciaccato	Playing a chord broken instead of together: *Similar to "arpeggio."*

acciaccatura	One or more grace notes played as quickly as possible as an ornament immediately before the principal note:

acciaio	Steel: *As in a steel beater for percussion.*
accompagnando	Accompanied
accopiato	Tying together
accorato	Sad, sorrowful
accordare	To tune
acuto	Sharp, piercing
adagio	Slowly: *See page 6.*
addolcimento	Sweetly, softening
addolorato	Sorrowfully
adiratamente	Angrily, furiously
ad libitum	(*ad lib.*) Freely, improvise: *Usually referring to tempo.*
a due; a2	Two players: *Refers to crash cymbals when used on cymbal parts.*
affabile	Gentle, gracefully
affannato	Distressed, anxious
affannoso	Breathless, anxious
affettuoso	Affectionate, with emotion
affezione	Tenderly, with affection
afflitto	Grieved, sorrowful
affrettato	Hurriedly, quickly

agevole	Easy, comfortable
aggiustamente	In strict tempo
aggressivo	Aggressive
agiatamente	Easily, with comfort
agiato	Comfortably, sedately
agilmente	With agility, nimbly
agitare	To shake (rub)
agitato	Agitated, excited
al	At the, to the, on the
alcuna(o)	Some, certain: *As "con alcuna licenza" (with some freedom).*
aleggiare	To flutter, vibrate irregularly
al fine	To the end
alla	To the, in the, at the
alla breve	Two beats to the measure: ¢
alla camera	Like chamber music
alla marcia	Like a March
alla militare	In a military style
alla moderna	In a modern style
allargando	(*allarg.*) To enlarge, growing slower
allegremente	Cheerfully, merrily
allegro	Fast, lively: *See page 7.*
allentando	Slackening, getting slower
allentato	Delayed, getting slower
allontanando; allantando	Dying away, *morendo*
allora	Then

alma, con	With soul, soulfully
alteramente	Haughty, proud, *maestoso*
alternando	Alternating
altezzosamente	Haughtily, proudly
alto	High, deep
altra(o)	Other, another
alzate	Raise, lift, to take off: *As in "alzate sordino" (take off mute).*
amabile	Tenderly, sweetly, lovely
amarevole	Bitterly, hatefully
almeno	At least
amorevole	Loving, lovely
amoroso	Fondly, with love
ampiezza	Breadth, broad
anacru'sis	(*Greek*) Upbeat to a measure
anche	Too, also
ancora	Again, yet, still (more)
andante; andando; andantino	Moderately slow, flowing: *See page 6 and 7.*
andantamente	Flowingly, smoothly
andare	To go, to walk
angoscioso	With anguish, grieved
anima, con	Soul, spirit, with feeling: *Anima is also the "sound post" of a string instrument.*
animato	Animated, lively
animoso	Animated, spirited
aperto	Open

appassionato	Impassioned, with passion
appena	Scarcely, hardly
appoggiate	To lean on or give support
appoggiatura	A grace note with a distinct harmonic application (different from an ornament): *This grace note is played on the beat and takes half of the following note value.*

a punta(o) d'arco	With the point (tip) of the bow: *For string instruments. See page 210.*
appunto	Exactly, precisely
arbitrio	Freely, at your pleasure
archi	String instruments
arco	With the bow: *For string and percussion instruments.*
ardent(e)	Fiery, passionate
ardito	Bold, daring
ardore, con	With warmth
arioso	Melodious, graceful, airy
armonici	Harmonics
arpeggio	Notes played in rapid succession:

articolato	Articulate, distinct
asprezza	Harshness, roughness

aspro	Harsh, piercing
assai	Very, very much
assoloto	Absolute
assordante	Deafening
astuto	Sharp, bright
a tempo	At the preceding tempo: *See page 8.*
attacca	To continue without pause
austero	Strict, severe
avvivando	Animated, lively

B

bacchetta	Drum stick, baton
baldamente	Boldly, courageously
balzato	Leaping, springing, jumping
barbaro	Barbaric, savage
batteria	Percussion section
battimenti, senza	Without beats or pulse: *Non mesura.*
battuta	Beat, downbeat
bellezza, con	With beauty, charming
bellicose	Warlike
ben(e)	Good, well: *As in "ben marc" (well marked).*
bianco	Half note: ♩ *The half note is also called "minima."*
biecamente	Grimly, stern
bis	Twice

16

bisbigliando	Whispering
biscroma	Thirty-second note: ♪
bizzaro	Fantastic, spirited
bocca chiusa	Humming: *Singing with closed lips.*
bocchino	Mouthpiece of a wind instrument
borbottando	As in rapid speech, muttering
bravura	Brilliance, boldness
breve	Double-whole note: ▭
brève	Short, brief
breve, alla	In "cut time:" ₵ *Two beats to the measure.*
brillante	Sparkling, brilliant
brio, con	With spirit, animated
brioso	Spirited, vivacious
brivido	To shiver, shake
brusco	Abrupt, short
brutale	Harsh, savage
buffa(o)	Comic, funny
buio	Dark, gloomy
burla	To mock, scorn

C

cadenza	A virtuoso solo passage
cadenzato	Rhythmical

calando	Gradually diminishing in tempo and dynamic
calcando	Pressing on, moving forward, *accel.*
calma(o)	Calm, tranquil
calore, con	With warmth
cambia	To change: *A direction to change tuning or instruments.*
camminando	Walking, strolling: *An easy and gentle tempo.*
campana	Chimes, large bell
campanelli	Orchestra bells, *Glockenspiel*
cantabile	In a singing style
cantando	Ability to sing in tune
cantante	Singer
canterellare	To hum, humming
canticchiare	To hum, humming
cantino	The highest string on a violin
canto	Singing, song
capo	Beginning, head: *As in "Da capo," from the beginning of the movement.*
cappella, a	Unaccompanied vocal music
capriccioso	Whimsical, fanciful
carezzando	Caressingly
caricato	To affect or exaggerate
carità, con	With love, benevolence
cassa	Drum
cèdendo	Yielding, getting slower
celere	Quick, fast, rapid

centro, al	At the center
cesura; cæsura	A short break or pause: //
che	Who, whom, that, which, than
cheto	Quiet, tranquil, calm
chiamata	Curtain call: *As in "tace sino alla chiamata" (do not play until the curtain call).*
chiaro	Clear, bright
chiassoso	Noisy, turbulent, jazzy
chiave	The musical clef:

chiavi, con le	To depress the keys of woodwind instruments without playing
chiuso	Stopped: *To insert the hand into the bell of a French horn.*
circa	Around, about
clangorous	A resounding loud metallic ringing sound
col	With
colla parte	To follow the solo part
colpi(o)	Strike, blow, shoot: *As in "colpi di cannone" (shoot the cannon).*
come	As, how, like
come prima	As before, similar: *See page 8.*
come sopra	As above, as before
come sta	As written

cominico, tempo del	Beginning tempo
commovènte	Moving, emotional, touching
còmodo	Easy, leisurely
completo	Complete, whole
con	With
con brio	With spirit, animation
concitato	Agitated, excited
con calore	With warmth
con dolore	With sorrow
con forza	With force, strength
con fuoco	With fire
con grazia	With grace
con moto	With movement
consolante	Consoling, comforting
con sordino	With a mute
con spirito	With spirit
contemplativo	Reflective, pensive
copèrto	Muffled, dampened: *See page 140.*
corda	String instruments
corda, sulla I	For string instruments to play on the G string: *The Roman numerals I, II, III, IV determine which string to use.*
corda vuota	An open string: *See page 211.*
cornetta a pistoni	Cornet
corno	Horn

corno inglese	English horn
coro	Chorus, choir
corona	Pause, hold: ⌒ *Fermata.*
corrente	Running, flowing
corta(o)	Short, brief
crescendo	(*cresc.*) Increasing in loudness towards a climax: $<$
cristalino	Clear, transparent
croma	Eighth note: ♪
cupo	Dark, somber

D

da capo	(D.C.) An indication in a score or part to return to the beginning
dal segno	(D.S.) An indication in a score or part to return to the sign: 𝄋 *As in "dal segno al fine" (from the sign to the end).*
deciso	Decisively, resolutely
decrescendo	(*decresc.*) Decreasing in loudness: $>$
deficièndo	Dying away
del	Of the
deliberato	Deliberately
delicatezza	Delicate, gentle
delicato	In a delicate, refined style

21

deridere	Mocking
desiderare	Yearning, longing for
desolato	Desolate, woeful
desto	Lively, quick
dèstra	Right hand
determinato	Determined, resolute
devozione	With devotion
diesis	The sharp sign: ♯
difficile	Difficult
dignità, con	With dignity
diluendo	Fading away
diminuendo	(*dim.*) Diminishing in loudness
disarmonia	Discord
discreto	Discrete, moderate
disinvòlto	Unconstrained, free and easy
disperato	Desperate, hopeless
disperdere	Dying away
disprezzo, con	With contempt, scorn
dissonanza	Dissonance
distaccato	Detached, separated
distanza, a	In the distance (offstage)
disteso	Stretched out, relaxed, slower
distinto	Distinct, separated, set apart
diventando	Becoming, transforming
divisi	(*div.*) Divided: *Played by two players, not as double-stops. For strings, see page 211.*

dolce	Sweetly, gently
dolcezza, con	With sweetness, gentleness
dolènte	Sadly, sorrowfully
doloroso	Painful, sorrowful
dopo	After, later
doppio	Double: *See page 8.*
drammatico	Dramatic, exaggerated
due	Two
duolo	Grief, sorrow, pain
duramente	Harshly, severely
durezza	Harshness, relentlessness

E

ebbrezza, con	With bravado
ebollimento	Agitated, exuberant
eccitante; *eccitato*	Excited
eco	Echo
ed	And
elegante	Elegant, graceful
elevato	Noble, lofty
emozione	Emotion, feeling
energetico	Vigorous, energetic
enfasi, con	With emphasis
enfatico	Emphatic
entusiasmo, con	With enthusiasm

epico	Epic, heroic, stately
equabile	Evenly, uniform
eròico	Heroic, strong
esagerando	Exaggerate, overplay
esaltatissimo	Very excited
esatto	Exact, precise
esitante	Hesitant, to falter
espansivo	Expansive, exuberant
espirando	Expire, fading away
espressivo	(*espress.*) Expressively, with expression
estatico	Extreme emotional excitement
estinguendosi	Dying away, *morendo*
estinto	Barely audible
estremo	Extreme, drastic
esuberante	Joyously, boisterous
esultante	Rejoicing, delightful
evidente	Audible
evvivando	Cheering

F

facile	Easily, simple
fagotto	Bassoon
falsetto	An artificially high singing voice
fantasia	Fantasy, imagination
fantastico	Amazing, incredible

fastidio	Annoyance, aggravation
fastoso	Sumptuous, portentous
febbrile	Feverish, restless
fermamente	Firmly, steadfastly
fermata	To hold a tone or rest: ⌒ *Hold for an indeterminate amount of time — in orchestral music this is determined by the conductor.*
fermezza, con	With firmness, steadiness
fermo	Firm, steady
feròce	Fierce, wildly
fervido	Impassioned
fervore, con	With warmth, passion
festivo; festoso	Festive, merry
fiacco	Weak, tired
fiato	Wind: *As in wind instruments.*
fiero	Fierce, vigorous
finale	Last movement of a musical work
finalmente	Finally, eventually, at last
fine	The end
finezza, con	With finesse, elegance
fioritura; *fiorette*	Ornaments or embellishments: *See "acciaccatura" and "appoggiatura."*
fischiare	To whistle
fisso	Firm, steady
flautando	A flute-like tone: *For string players, tilt the bow in order to use less hair and play near the fingerboard. See page 212.*

flauto	Flute
flèbile	Feeble, plaintive, mournful
flessibile	Flexible, yielding
fluente	Flowing, smooth
fluido	Singing, *cantabile*
focoso	Fiery, forceful
forse	Maybe, perhaps
forte	*f* - Loud, strong
fortepiano	*fp* - Loud, then suddenly soft
fortissimo	*ff* - Very loud
fortississimo	*fff* - Very very loud
forza, con	With force
freddo	Cool, with indifference
frèmente	Furious, passionate
frenetico	Frenzied, frantic
fresco	Lively, vigorous
fretta, con	With haste, to hurry
frullato	Whirring, fluttering
fruscio	Whispering, sound of a "swish"
fuggevole	Fleeting, quickly passing
funereo	Funeral, gloomy
fuoco, con	With fire
fuori, di	From outside (backstage)
furioso	Furious, frantic
furore	Fury, passion

G

gagliardo	Vigorous, energetic
gaio	Joyful, cheerful
galòppo	Gallop, fast tempo
garbato	Pleasing, graceful
gaudioso	Joyful
gemendo	Lamenting, groaning
gentilmente	Gently, nobly
giocoso	Humorous, playful
giulivo	Joyful, cheerful
giusto	Strict, exact: *As in "tempo giusto" (in strict tempo).*
glissando	(*gliss.*) A rapid scale-like passage up or down: *Usually on a keyboard; however string, wind, and percussion players can also create this effect.*
glorioso	Glorious
goffaggine	Clumsy, awkward
gracile	Delicate, graceful
gradatamente	Gradually, step by step
gradevole	Pleasant, charming
gradito	Agreeably
grado a grado	Step by step
grande	Large, broad

grande pausa	(G.P.) Grand Pause. Indicated on parts, telling the player no one plays in this measure: *Usually played in tempo.*
grandezza	Grandeur, magnificent
grandioso	In a grand manner, majestic
grave	Solemn, serious
gravità	Seriousness, deepness of sound, dignified
grazioso	Gracefully, elegantly
grido	Crying out, shout
grossolano	Unrefined, vulgar, rude
grottescamente	Grotesque, ridiculous
gruppetto	A turn: *A group of grace notes (normally 4) following a given pitch, including the note above, the note itself, the note below, and again, the note itself.*

guerra	War like, martial
gusto, con	With good taste

I

ieratico	Irregular, capricious
imitando	Imitate, mimic
immobile	Motionless, stationary
impavido	Bold, brave

imperioso	Commanding, stately
impeto, con	Impetuous, with a driving force
impetuoso	Violent, impulsive
imponènte	Imposing, impressive
incalzando	Pressing, moving forward
incantando	Enchanting, charming
inciso	Incisive, sharp
indifferente	Indifferent, unenthusiastic
indistinto	Indistinct, blurred, faint
indolente	Insensitive, lazy
indugiando	To drag, holding back
inflessione	Inflection, flexible: *To change the character of a rhythm or pitch.*
infuorandosi	To enrage, infuriate
ingenuità	Simple, naive, natural
iniziale	Initial, original: *As "in tempo."*
inquièto	Restless, agitated
insensibilmente	Lacking delicacy or refinement
insidoso	Treacherous, seductive
insinuante	To allude, suggest
insistenza	To insert, introduce
intensificando	To intensify, increase dynamic
intenzionato	Deliberate, intentional
intrepido	Fearless, brave
invocando	To bring about, put into effect
ipnoticamente	Hypnotic
irato	Irate, angry

ironico	Ironic, dry, wry
irrequieto	Restless, nervous
irresoluto	Hesitating
irritato	Irritate, enrage, excite
islancio, con	With élan, lively
istesso	The same tempo: *Similar to "l'istesso tempo."*

L

lacerante	Tearing, violent
lacrimoso	Tearful, mournful
lagnoso	Wailing, groaning
lamentoso	Plaintive, mournful
lancio, con	With forward motion
languendo	Fading away
largamente	Broad, sustained
larghetto	Slightly faster than largo: *See page 6.*
largo	Slow tempo, broadening: *See page 6.*
lasciare	To let, leave
legatura	A slur: ⌒
legato	Smooth and connected: *Indicated by a slur.*

leggiardo	Graceful, charming

leggiero	Lightly, airy
legni	Woodwinds
legno	Wood
legno, col	For strings, play with the wood of the bow: *See page 212.*
legno, il	The woodwind section of the orchestra
legnoso	Woody, stiff
lène	Soft, faint, breathless
lenemente	Slowly
lenezza	Faintly, mellow
lèntando	Growing slower
lento	Slowly: *See page 6.*
lésto	Swift, quick
letargico	Lethargic, drowsy
levare	To lift or take off: *As in mutes.*
lezioso	Sympathetic, sorrowful
liberamente	Freely
licènza	License, liberty, *ad lib.*
lieto	Happy, joyful
lieve	Gentle, delicate
limpedo	Clear, bright, transparent
lirico	Lyrical, operatic
liscio	Smooth: *Similar to "legato."*
l'istesso	The same (tempo): *See page 8.*
loco	As written, return to normal position
lontano	In the distance: *Off stage.*

lugubre	Mournful, gloomy
luminoso	Brilliance, clarity
lunga(o)	Prolonged, hold
lusingando	Caressing
lusinghiero	Flattering, alluring
luttuoso	Mournful, sad

M

ma	But
maestoso	Majestic, stately
maggiore	Major tonality
magico	Magical
malinconico	Melancholy, sadness
malizioso	Malicious, mischievous
mancando	Becoming less, fading away
manico	Fingerboard of string instruments
maniera	Manner, style
mano destra	Right hand
mano sinistra	Left hand
marcare	To bring out
marcia	In the style of a March
marcato	(*marc.*) Marked, pronounced
martellato	A short, heavy accent: *Also called a "heavy wedge." See page 213.*

marziale	Martial, March like
massiccio	Massive, heavy
meccanico	Mechanical, unemotional
medesimo	The same
media(o)	Medium
meditabondo	Thoughtful, dreamily
meditativo	Meditative, pensive
melodia	Melody
melodico	Melodious, tuneful
meno	Less
meravigliato	Amazing, astonished
messa	Mass
mesto; *mestamente*	Mournful, sad
metà	Half: *As in "la metà pizz." (half the section plays pizzicato).*
metallico	Metallic, brassy
mettalizzare i suoni	To play with a "brassy" tone
mezza(o)	Half
mezzo forte	*mf* - Medium loud
minaccioso	Threatening, ominous
minima	Half note: ♩
minore	Minor tonality
misterioso	Mysterious
mistico	Mystical
misura	Meter, beat

33

misurato	Measured, strict time
mite	Quiet, gentle
mobile	Flexible, yielding
moderato	Moderately: *See page 7.*
modificazioni, senza	Without modification, as written
mòdo	Manner, style: *As in "mòdo ordinario" (ordinary manner).*
molezza, con	With flexibility, supple
mòlle	Soft, delicate, languid
molto	Very, much
monotamente	Without emotion, serious
mòrbido	Soft, tender
morboso	Morbid, gloomy
mordente	Biting, sharp
mordènte	Mordent: *A musical ornament.*

Mordent   Inverted Mordent

morendo	Dying away
mormorando	Murmuring, whispering
mosso	Moving, with motion: *"Meno mosso" (less motion) or "più mosso" (more motion).*
motivo conduttore	A musical motive or theme: *"Leitmotiv" in German.*
moto, con	With motion, moving ahead
movendo	Moving faster

34

movimento	Movement, motion, *più mosso*
muta; mutano	Change: *A directive to change key or pitch. Frequently used for French horn and timpani.*
mutamento	Change, variation

N

naturale	Natural style: *Without ornaments or without mute.*
nervosa	Nervous, spirited, excited
net; netto	Distinct, sharp
niènte	Nothing, as in barely audible
nòbilemente	Noble, refined, dignified
non	Not: *As in "non troppo" (not too much).*
normale	Normal, ordinary
nostaligico	Sentimental, yearning
nuovo, di	Again, once more

O

obbligato	Obligatory, indispensable: *When a part is special or unusual and must be played.*
occorrere	As needed or required
od	Or
ogni	Every, each
ondeggiando	A tremolo or vibrato
ondulato	Regarding a rippling effect

opprimente	Heavy, oppressive
oramai	Now, by this time
ordinario	Ordinary, as usual
orgoglioso	Proud, glorious
orribile	Horrible, nasty
oscuro	Obscure, sinister
osservato	As noted, play as written
ossessivo	Obsessive, compulsive
ossia; ovvero	Or, in place of: *An alternative version. See page 213.*
ostinato	Obstinate: *Continuous repetition of a theme.*
ottava alta	One octave higher
ottava bassa	One octave lower
ottavino	Piccolo
ottoni	Brass section

P

pacato	Peaceful, serene
paio	Pair
palpitante	Passionate, heart-throbbing
parlando	Recitative: *In a speaking style.*
parte, colla	With the part: *Follow along with the solo part.*
passionato	Impassioned, with emotion
pastoso	Soft, with a mellow tone

patètico	Affectionate, tender
patimento	Suffering, grief
pauroso	Fearful, apprehensive
pausa	A short stop or pause: **'**
penetrante	Sharp, piercing
penosamente	Painful, troublesome
pensoso	Thoughtful, serious
penultimo	Penultimate: *Next to the last (measure).*
per	For, by, in order to
percosso	To strike, hit, or clash
perdendosi	Fading away: *Becoming slower and softer.*
perdutamente	Desperately, hopelessly
pèrfidio	Treacherous, wickedness
però	However, yet, but
perpetuo	Unceasing, constant
pesante; pesato	Heavy, weighty
petulanza, con	With arrogance, irritable
pezzo	A piece, part, or composition
piacere, a	At your pleasure, as you wish
piacevole	Pleasing, charming, agreeable
pianamente	Smoothly, softly
piangendo	Weeping, tearful, plaintive
pianissimo	*pp* - Very soft
pianississimo	*ppp* - Very very soft
piano	*p* - Soft

piatti	Cymbals: *A generic term that does not specify whether to use a suspended cymbal or a pair of crash cymbals.*
picchettato	Detached, *staccato*
piccolo	Little, small
pieghevole	Flexible, yielding
pienamente	Fully, with fullness
pietoso	Tenderly, compassionate
pigrizia	Slow, lazy
più	More
pizzicato	(*pizz.*) Plucking the string of a string instrument
placabile	Mildly, soothing
placare	To calm or soothe
placido	Calm, peaceful
pochissimo	As little as possible
pòco	Little: *As in "pòco più mosso"* (*a little faster*).
pòco a pòco	Little by little: *As in a cresc., dim., accel., rit.*
pòco meno	A little less
pòco più	A little more
poesia	Lyrical, with emotion
poi	Then, next, later
pollice, col	With the thumb
pomposo	Pompous, majestic

ponticèllo, sul	Near the bridge on string instruments: *To play near the bridge with the bow — producing a glassy tone. See page 214.*
portamento	1. For string players, this means to slide from one note to another sounding all notes in between: *See page 214.*

2. For woodwind and brass players this implies connecting notes in a sustained and *legato* manner.

portando	Sustaining: *As in "legato."*
portato	Well-articulated: *Sometimes thought of as a half staccato and half legato.*

possible	Possible, conceivable, likely
precedente	Precede, come before
precipitando	Rushing ahead, hurrying
precipitoso	Rush, rushed
preciso	Precise, exact
preghevole	To plead, entreat, or request
pressante	Pressing on: *As in "accel."*
prestissimo	Extremely fast: *See page 7.*
presto	Very fast: *See page 7.*

prima(o)	First, principal, original
primitive	Primitive, crude
principale	Master, main, chief
principio	Beginning, start
produrre un suono metallico	To blow strongly, to force the tone on brass instruments
profundo	Profound, deep, intense
prolungando	Prolong, extend, sustain
pronto	Quickly
pronunciato	Pronounce, articulate
prorompendo	Bursting forth, breaking out
prudentemente	Prudently, cautiously
pugno	Fist
pulsando	Pulsating, throbbing
pungente	Sharp, piercing
puntato	Referring to notes being played in a *staccato* manner
punto	Point: *As in "al punto" (at the point of the bow). See page 214.*

Q

quanto	How much, how many
quasi	Almost, nearly
quattro	Four
questo	This
quieto	Quiet, tranquil

R

rabbia, con	With rage or fury
raccontando	Narrated
raddolcendo	To soften or smooth
raddoppiando	Doubling
raffrenando	Holding back, getting slower
raggiungere	To reach, to arrive at
rallentando	Slowing down in tempo: *Usually not as dramatic as a ritard.*
rapidamente	Rapidly, quickly
rapido	Rapid, fast
rapsodico	Expressive and romantic music
rassegnato	Resigned, hopeless
rasserenandosi	Brightening, with serenity
rattenendo	Restrained, holding back
rauco	Harsh, strident
ravviando	Lively, jazzy
recitando	Reciting, acting, performing
recitative	To sing or speak out of tempo and rhythm
religioso	In a religious, devotional manner
replica	Repetition, repeat
respingendo	Holding back
respiro	Breath, breathing
ridendo	Laughing

rigido	Rigid, unbending
rigo	Music staff or line
rigoglioso	Exuberant, joyously
rigoroso	Strictly in time, rigorous
rilasciando	To relax, slacken, slow down
rilievo	With emphasis, importance
rimbrottando	In a harsh or severe manner
rimettendosi	Going back, resuming: *As in a slower tempo or earlier section.*
rinforzando; *rinforzato*	(*rinf.*) To reinforce, accent: *Operates within a given dynamic level — usually not a dynamic level by itself.*
ripetizione	Repetition, repeat
ripigliando	Resuming, to begin again
riposo, con	Restfully, calmly
riprendendo	To start, to go back
ripresa	Repeat of a section of a composition
risentito	Resentful, angry
riservato	To hold back, *rit.*
risoluto	Determined, resolved
risonare; *risonante*	Resounding, sonorous
risvegliato	Rousing, exciting
ritardando	(*rit.*or *ritard.*) Slowing down, little by little
ritenuto	Held back, *rit.*
ritmico	Rhythmical
ritmo	Rhythm

ritornando	Returning, going back
riverbero	Reverberation, echo
robusto	Strong, vigorous
roco	Hoarse
rombando	Humming
rubato	Freely: *To slow down or speed up the tempo at the discretion of the player or conductor.*
rustico	Folksy, simple
ruvido	Course, rough

S

saltando; saltato	A general term for bowed string instruments to play off the string: *See page 215.*
saltellante	Skipping, hopping
sardonico	Scornful, sneering, satiric
sassofone	Saxophone
satanico	Wicked, satanic
satirico	Satirical, biting
scacciapensieri	Jew's harp: *See "ribeta" on page 148.*
scampanio	Continuous ringing of bells or chimes
scatenato	To let loose, wild
scattando	Sudden movement, outburst

scherzando; scherzoso	Playfully, lightly
scherzo	Jokingly, humorous: *See page 8.*
schiamazzando	Continuous squawking, constant din
schianto	A sudden crash or burst of sound
schietto	Straightforward, plainly
scioltamente	Freely, easily
scivolando	A glissando
scolpito	Clearly, distinctly
scomparendo	Disappearing, vanishing
scoperto	Uncovered, take off mute: *As in not muted or dampened.*
scordato	Out of tune
scordatura	To purposely retune a string instrument for a special effect: *See "heraustimmen" on page 229.*
scorrevole	Gliding, flowing
scucito	Detached, separated: *The opposite of "legato."*
scuro	Gloomy, sinister
sdegnoso	Rude , overbearing
secco	(*sec.*) Short, dry
seconda	Second: *As in "seconda volta" (second time).*
segno	Sign: 𝄋 *As in "Del Segno" (to the sign).*
segue	That which follows without pause
seguendo	Following

selvaggio	Wild, primitive, barbaric
semibiscroma	Sixty-fourth note: 𝅘𝅥𝅱
semibreve	Whole note: **o**
semicroma	Sixteenth note: 𝅘𝅥𝅯
semiminima	Quarter note: 𝅘𝅥
semplice	Simple, plain
sèmpre	Always
sensibile	Sensible, sensitive
sentimento, con	With feeling, emotion
sentito	With feeling, sensitive
senza	Without
separato	Separated, detached
sereno	Serene, tranquil
serietà; serioso	Serious, dramatic
sestetto	Sextet
settimino	Septet
severo	Strict, severe
sfida	With defiance, exaggerated
sfiorato	Caressing, with a light touch
sfogato	Airy, light and easy touch
sfoggiando	Excessive display
sfolgorante	Flashing, dazzling
sforzando; sforzato	(*sfz*) Forceful: *Adding a strong emphasis to a given note — stronger than an accent. Usually performed within a given dynamic.*

sforzare la nota	To blow strongly, to force the tone
sfrenato	Unrestrained, run amok
sfumare; sfumato	To disappear, to tone down
sguaiato	Coarse, unrefined
sibillino	Mysterious
sicurezza, con	With assurance, security
silènzio	Silence
sillabato	Articulate
simile	(*sim.*) Similar
sin(o)	Until, up to, as far as
sinistra, mano	Left hand
sipario	Stage curtain
slancio, con	With spirit, momentum
slargando	Slowing down
slentando	Becoming slower
smanioso	Raging, frenzy
smaritto	Bewildered, frightened
sminuendo	Diminishing, getting softer
smorendo	Dying away
smorzando	Extinguishing, dying away
snèllo	Nimble, graceful
soave	Sweetly, gently
sòffice	Soft, tender
soffocato	Dampened, muffled
sognando	Dreamy, longing
solenne	Solemn, serious
solito	Common, ordinary, as usual

sonabile	Playable
sonatore	Performer, musician
sonoro	Sonorous, resonant
sopra	Above, before, previous: *As in "come sopra" (as before).*
sordamente	To play in a muted or muffled style
sordino	Muted, with a mute
sordo	Dull
sospirando	Sighing, plaintive
sostenuto	(*sost.*) Sustained
sotto	Under, below
sottovoce	Undertone, under the breath
sovrapposto	Non-arpeggio: *A chord played simultaneously.*
sparire	Disappear, vanish, fading away
spavalderia	Arrogance, boastfulness
spaziato	Wandering
spazzola	Wire brushes
spegnendosi	Extinguish, dying away
spegnere	To stop or dampen: *As in "spegnere il suono" (stop the sound).*
spensieratamente	Without thought, freely
speranza, avec	Hopelessly
spèrdendosi	Dispersed, fading away
spianato	Smooth, sustained, *legato*

spiccato	A technique for string instruments by rapidly bouncing the bow on the strings: *Usually played in the center portion of the bow. See page 216.*
spiegato	Allowing the sound to unfold, open
spietato	Cold, ruthless
spigliatezza	Ease, agility
spigliato	Easy, free
spingendo	Pushing ahead
spirando	Breathing, expiring
spirito, con	With spirit, animated
spronato	Spurred, clawed
squillante	Shrill, piercing
stabilimento	Established, settled
staccato	(*stac.*) Detached, separated: *See page 216.*

stanco	Tired, dragging
stendendo	Extending, *rallentando*
stentando; stentato	Labored, holding back
stentòrius	Extremely loud
steso	Spreading out, slower
stesso	The same
stile	Style, character
stinguendo	Fading away
stiracchiando	To stretch out, slowing down

stizzoso	Angry, irritable
stonare	To sing off pitch
strappare	To rip or tear: *A strong down-bow or pizzicato attack for strings. See page 216.*
strascicando	Dragging, drawing out
stravaganza	Extravagantly
straziante	Distressing, agonizing
strepitoso	Noisy, boisterous
strette(o)	Hurried, pressed together
stridente	Sharp, shrill, clashing
stringendo	Pressing forward, faster
strisciando; *strisciato*	To glide from one note to another: *As in a "glissando."*
strumenti *musicale al fiato*	Woodwind instruments
strumento	Musical instrument
suadente	In a persuasive manner
subito	(*sub.*) Suddenly, quickly
sul	On the, near the
suonare	To sound or play
suonare a fantasia	To improvise
suonare fuori tono	To play out of tune
suonare in tono	To play in tune
suonare reale; *suoni reali*	Actual pitch
sonare troppo alto *rispetto al tono*	To play sharp

suonare troppo basso rispetto al tono	To play flat
suono armonioso	Musical sound
sussurro	Whispering
svanendo	Vanish, disappear, fading away
svegliando	Aroused, awakened
svelto	Quick, swift, lively

T

tacet; tace	Silence: *This can refer to an entire movement or the remainder of a movement as in "tacet al fine."*
tagliente	Sharp, harsh
tallone, al	At the heel of the bow: *Also called the "nut" or "frog" of the bow. See page 217.*
tamburo	Drum
tanto	Much, many, so much
tappato	Stopped: *To insert the hand into the bell of a French horn.*
tardamente	Slowing down, *rit.*
tastiera, sulla; tasto, sul	For string players to lightly bow over the fingerboard: *Producing a flute-like effect. See page 217.*
tema	Theme
tempestoso	Stormy, raging
tempo	Rate of speed in music

tempo, a	The original tempo
tempo mark	Indicates the rate of speed and character of the music: *Ex. Allegro maestoso.*
tenacemente	Persistently, tenaciously
tenebroso	Dark, gloomy
tenendo	Sustaining
teneramente	Tenderly, with tender emotion
tenero	Tender, loving
tenuto	(*ten.*) To hold, make important: *An articulation, adding a long stress accent to a note. This does not actually affect the note value — it exaggerates the note with a gentle, sustained accent.*

teso	Nervous, tense
tessitura	The range covering the notes of a given part
tetro	Dark, somber
timbro	Sound, tone color: *Same as "timbre" in French.*
timido	Timid, shy, bashful
timoroso	Timidly, hesitantly
tinto, con	With shading, expressive
tirare in su	To slide upwards
toccata	Touch, touching
tocco	The touch or attack

togliere la sordina	Take off mute
tonante	Thundering
tòno	Tone, key, pitch
torbido	Cloudy, gloomy
tornando	Returning, going back
tostamente	Quickly, rapidly
tòsto	Quick, rapid
tradotto;	Arranged, transposed
traduzione	
tragico	Tragic
tranquillo	Peaceful, calm, serene
trascinando	To drag, hold back
trasognato	Dreamy
trasparente	Clear, transparent
trasporto	Enthusiastic
trattenuto	To hold back, *rit.*
tre	Three
tremolo	Rapid alternation of a tone
trepidamente	Anxiously, trembling
trillo	A trill, rapid alternation of two tones
trionfale;	Triumphal, triumphant
trionfante	
triste	Sad, melancholy
tristo	Wicked, wretched
tromba	Trumpet
troncare	To stop, cut off
troppo	Too much

tumultuoso	Commotion, agitated
tutta; tutte; tutti	All, all together
tutta forza	With full power or strength

U

udibile	Audible
uguaglianza	Equality, balance, sameness: *As in "con perfette uguaglianza" (perfectly even).*
uguale	Equal, identical, the same
ultima(o)	Ultimate, final
umore, con	With humor
un; una; uno	A, one
unisono	(*unis.*)To play together or revoke a directive: *Such as "divisi."*

V

va	To go on
vagaroso	Wandering, rambling
vaghezza, con	With charm
vago	Vague, elusive
valore	Time value: *As in doppio valore" (twice as slow as the previous time value).*
vaporoso	Hazy, misty, transparent
variazione	Variation
veemènza	Impetuous, passionate

velare	Veiled, subdued, muffled
veloce	Rapid, swiftly
ventile	Valve horn
venusto	Beautiful, elegant
vezzoso	Charming, graceful
vibrante	Vibrating, pulsating
vibrato	A wavering effect of the tone
vicino	Near, close by
vieppiù	Much more
vigoroso	Vigorous, with energy
violènte	Violent, furious
violino	Violin
violino de spalla	Concertmaster
violoncello	Cello
virtuoso	A highly-proficient musician
vista, a	Sight reading
vita	Lively, animated
vivace	Brisk, lively: *See page 8.*
vivènte	Alive, lively
vivezza	Lively, animated
vivido	Vigorous
vivo	Alive, quick
voce	Voice
voglia	Longing, sensual
volando; volante	Flying, fast
volata	A rapid run or passage
volgare	Vulgar, course

volontà, a	At your pleasure
vòlta	Turning, time, direction: *As in "prima vòlta" (1ˢᵗ time).*
vòlta subito	(V.S.) Turn the page quickly
voluttuoso	Voluptuous, sensual
vuota	Empty (Grand Pause)

Musical Directives – French

A

abandon, avec	With abandon, freedom
accelerer(ez)	To accelerate, quicken
accentuer	To stress, emphasize
accompagnement	Accompaniment
accorder	To tune an instrument
accouplé	Connected, *legato*
accrochez	Attach
à demi-jeux	With half the power
à demi-oix	With half the voice, whispering
à deux	With two players on the same part
à deux cordes	On two strings
à deux mains	For two hands
à deux temps	In cut-time: 𝄵
adoucissant	Soothing, mellow
affable	Pleasing
affaiblir	To grow fainter, fade away
affectueusement	Affectionately
agile	Agility, nimble
agilité, avec	With agility
agité	Restless, agitated

agiter	To shake (rub)
agréable	Pleasantly
agréments	Ornaments or embellishments: *See "acciaccatura" and "appoggiatura" in Italian on pages 12 and 15.*
aigre; aigu	Piercing, sharp, high pitched
aisance, avec	With ease
aisé	Easy, comfortable
alerte	Agile, lively
allant	Going on, continuing
allègre	Lively, cheerful
Allemand	German
allez	To go on
allongé	Prolonged, hold
alto	Viola
ample; amplement	Broadly, sonorous, ample
anacrouse	Upbeat: *From the Greek "anacru'sis."*
anche	A reed: *Used in the mouthpiece of wind instruments.*
angoissé	Anguished, distressed
animant; animé	Lively, animated: *See page 9.*
aplomb	Steady
appuyer	To support or stress
après	After
apreté	Harshly, sharp
archet	Bow for string instruments
ardent	Fiery, *con fuoco*

argentin	Silvery, smooth
arpège	Broken chord, *arpeggio*:

arpège descendant	Descending chord, *arpeggio*:

arraché	To tear or rip: *A strong down-bow or pizzicato attack for strings. See page 218.*
arrêter	To stop, cut off
articulé	Articulated
assez	Enough, quite, rather, fairly: *As in "assez vite" (fairly quick).*
attendre	To wait, pause
attendri	Tenderly, moving
attenuer	To become softer, to fade away
au	On, to, in, at
aucun	Any, none
audacieux	Boldly, daring
augmentant l'intensite, en	Becoming louder
au pas	Strictly in tempo
aussi	Too, also
aussitôt	Immediately, *subito*
autant que	As much as
autre	Other

avant	Before, previous to
avec	With
avisé	Sensible, prudent

B

badin	Playful, light-hearted
badinage	Jokingly, with humor
baguette	Drum stick
baisser l'accord	For string players; a request to purposely retune a string for a special effect: *See "heraustimmen" on page 229.*
balancement	Tremolo:

bariolage	A technique for string instruments: *See page 219.*
bâton	The stick used by conductors for directing the orchestra
battement, sans	Without beats or pulse: *Non mesura.*
batterie	Percussion section
battre	To beat: *As in "battre le mesure" (to beat time).*
beaucoup	Very much
bécarre	The natural sign: ♮
belliqueux	Combative, warlike

bémol	The flat sign: ♭
bien	Fine, good, well
bis	Twice: *Generally used to repeat a measure or passage.*
bizarre	Fanciful, bizarre
blanche	Half note: ♩
bois	Wood, woodwind instruments
bois, le	The woodwind section of the orchestra
bondissant	Bouncing, skipping
bonheur	Happily, joyous
bord, au	At the edge
bouché; bouchez	Stopped: *To modify the tone of a French horn by inserting the hand into the bell.*
bouche fermée	Singing or humming with a closed mouth
bourrasque	Stormy, gusty
bravoure	Brilliant, *bravura, bravo*
bref; brève	Short
brilliant	Sparkling, brilliant
brisé	Detached, broken: *As in an arpeggio or short, detached strokes with the violin bow.*
broderies	Ornaments or embellishments: *See "acciaccatura" and "appoggiatura" in Italian on pages 12 and 15.*
bruit	Sound, noise

C

caché	Muffled, subtle
cadencé	Rhythmically
caisse	Drum
calmant, en	Calm, soothing
calme	Calm, quiet, tranquil
capricieux	Capricious, whimsical
caressant, en	Caressingly, affectionate
carillon	Orchestra bells
cédant, en; cédez	To give way, get slower
céleste	Heavenly
césure	A short break or pause: //
chaleur, avec	Warmth, lovingly
chalumeau	Low register of the clarinet
changer	To change, exchange
chanson; chant; chantant	A song, singing
chanterelle	The highest string of the violin
chaque	Each, every
charme, avec	With charm, gracefully
chatoyant	Shimmering, sparkling
chaud	Warm, sensitive
chauffez	Excited, animated
chevalet	The bridge of a string instrument: *See page 219.*

chevrotant	Trembling, shaking (trill)
choeur	Chorus, choir
chuchotant; *chuchoter*	Whisper, murmur
cinglant	Violent, bitterly
clair	Clear, brilliant
clef de fa	Bass Clef: 𝄢
clef de sol	Treble clef: 𝄞
cloche	Chimes, large bell
colère	Anger, wrath
comique	Comical, humorous
comme	As, like
comme au dessus	As above
comme *auparavant*	As before
comme avant	As above, as before
commencer	Start, begin
commodément	Comfortably
compter	To count measures until re-entry
confus	Blurred, vague
conserver	Retain, keep
continu	Continued, ongoing
contre	Against
cor	A horn, French horn
cor anglais	English horn
corde	String, string instruments

corde à jour;	Open string: *See "corda vuota" on page*
corde à vide	*211.*
cornet à pistons	Cornet
corps de	Crook of a brass instrument
rechange	
cor simple	A natural horn
coulant, en	Flowing, gliding
coulè	Slur: ⌒
coulisse	A glissando for wind instruments
coup	To hit, strike
coup d'archet	A stroke of the bow
coupure	A "cut:" *Music omitted in a score or part.*
courroux	Anger, wrath
court	Short: *As in "très court" (very short).*
couvert	Covered, muffled, snares off
croche	Eighth note: ♪
cuivrer le sons	To blow strongly, to force the tone: *To play with a "brassy" tone.*
cuivres	Brass instruments, the brass section

D

dans	In
davantage	More
de	From, of
début	Beginning, start
déchirant	Piercing, tearing

décidé	Determined, resolved
découplé	Separated or detached, *staccato*
décrochez	Detached
défaillant	Weakening, dying away
défi	Challenging, defiant
dehors, en	To stand out, emphasize: *For string instruments to play over the fingerboard. See page 220.*
délicat	Delicate, sensitive
délices	Delightful, pleasing
délié	Separated notes: *As in "staccato."*
délirer	Wild, delirious, frenzied
demi, à	Half, in the middle
demi-jeu	To play at half the dynamic
demi-pause	Half rest
demi-teinte	Half tone, shaded, softer
demi-ton	Semitone
demi-voix	Half voice, softer
dernier	Last, final
derrière	Behind
des	From
désaccouplé	Separated or detached
désespoir	Despair, hopelessness
désordonné	Disorderly, chaotic
dessus	Over, above, upper part
détaché	Separated or detached: *See page 220.*
détaché sec	Very separated or detached

détendre; *détendu*	Relaxed, slower
détonner	To sing off pitch
deux	Two
deux temps	Cut time, two beats in the measure: ₵
devant	Before
diaphane	Transparent, clear
dièse	The sharp sign: ♯
difficile	Difficult
dignità, avec	With dignity
diminuant, *en le son*	Becoming softer, fading away
discordance	Discord
discrètment	Secretively, unobtrusively
disparaissant, *en*	Disappearing, fading away
disperser	Disperse, dying away
dissonance	Dissonance
distinct	Clear, well marked
divisès, en	Played by two players
doigt	Finger, fingering
dolent	Mournful, full of grief
double	Mordent:

Upper Mordent   Lower (Inverted) Mordant

double-croche	Sixteenth note: ♪
doucement	Gently, smoothly
douloureux	Sad, painful
douce; doux	Soft, sweet, gentle
du	Of the, any, some
d'une maniére solennelle	Solemnly
dur	Hard
dureté	Harshness, relentlessness

E

eblouisant	Dazzling, stunning
echappée	An ornamentation:

May also mean the dramatic release of a phrase.

échelle	The scale
écho	Like an echo
èclatant	Sparkling, brilliant
éclat, avec	Dramatically, with great pomp
effacer	Fading away, *morendo*
effleurer	With a very light touch
égal	Equal, steady

egalement; 　*égalité*	Evenly
élan, avec	With enthusiasm, passion
élargissant, en	To expand, *allargando*
elegance, avec	Elegantly, gracefully
eloigner	To grow more distant, *morendo*
emouvant	Arousing emotion
emphase, avec	With emphasis, accent
emporté	Angry, fiery
empressé	Hurrying, moving faster
ému	With feeling, emotion
en	In, to
enchainez	Link together, *segue*
encore	Again, more, over and over
énergie, avec	With energy
énervant	Irritating, annoying
énigmatique	Mysterious
enjoué	Playful, lighthearted
enlever la 　*sourdine*	Take off mute
entêtement	Persistent, determined
enthousiasme	Enthusiastic, zest
entint	Dull, *non vibrato*
entrain	With spirit, drive
entrée	Overture
enveloppé	Covered, muffled
éperdu	Violent, frantic

épuisement	With exhaustion, fatigue
estompé	Blurred, gently blending into a thinner sound
éteignant	Fading, dying away
éteint	Off
étendu	Broad, wide
étincelant	Brilliant
étonnement	Surprise, astonishment
étouffé	To muffle, dampen
éveillé	Active, alert
exaggération	Exaggerate
excessivement	Excessively, extremely
excite	Excited, agitated
executants	Performers
expressif	Expressive
extase	Ecstasy
extatique	Ecstatic, rapturous

F

facile	Easy, effortless
façon, sans	Without ceremony, simply
faire ressortir	To bring out
fantaisie	Fantasy, whimsical
farouche	Wild
fausse; faux	False
fausset	Falsetto: *Artificially high singing voice.*

ferme	Firm, steady
fervent	Great warmth of feeling
ferveur, avec	Fervently
feu, avec	With fire, passion
fier	Majestic, *maestoso*
fin	End
finalement	Eventually, finally
finement	Delicately, finely
flageolet	For string instruments, to play harmonics: *See page 220.*
flotter	To float, vacillate
flou	Hazy, blurry
fluide	Fluid, flowing, smooth
fouetté	Whipping the bow: *Accent on an up bow with energy.*
frappe	To strike, to attack
frénétique	Madly, rage
fròler	To brush slightly (rub)
fulgurant	Dazzling, brilliant
funébre	Funeral, mournful
furieuement; furieux	Furiously
furtif	Stealthy, sneaky
fuyant	Evasive, fleeing

G

gai(e)	Merry, lively, brisk
gallop, au	A lively dance in 2/4 time
genou	Knee: *As in "avec le genou" (with the knee). Using both the knee and fist to execute rapid rhythms on a tambourine.*
gentiment	Gently
glissé; glizzez	Glissando: *A rapid, up or down, scale-like passage.*
grâce, avec	With charm, grace
gracieux	Graceful
grave	Serious, solemn: *See page 9.*
gros	Big, rough, massive
grossiérement	Rough, rudely
grossissant	Becoming slower: *Similar to "largamente" in Italian.*
guilleret	Jolly, lively

H

haletant	Breathlessly, panting
hâte, avec	Accelerate, with haste
haut	High
hautbois	Oboe
hauteur réelle	Sounds as written

héroïque	Heroic, noble
hésitant	Hesitate, delayed
heurté	To hit, strike, clash
humeur, avec	With humor, amusing

I

impérieux	Pressing, urgent
impétueux	Impetuous, headstrong
implacable	Unrelenting, remorseless
improvisant, en	Improvising
incisive	Sharp, biting
incolore	Bland, boring
indécis	Indecisive, hesitant
indifferent	Indifferent, boring
indiqué	Indicate
indolence, avec	Lethargic
inflexible	Unyielding, rigid
innocemment	Simple, without emotion
inquiet	Uneasy, anxious
intimement	Intimately
irisé	Iridescent, colorful
ironique	Ironic, humorous, sarcastic
irrationnel	Lopsided, unequal
irréelment	Dreamlike
irritant	Angry, irritated

J

jante, sur la	On the rim
jeté	A thrown-bow technique: *Using the upper part of the bow rebounding several times with a down-bow motion. See page 221.*
jeu; jouée; jouer	To play
joliment	Prettily, nicely
jouer faux	To play out of tune
jouer juste	To play in tune
jouer trop bas	To play flat
jouer trop haut	To play sharp
joyeux	Joyous, festive
jusqu'à	Until, up to

L

l'aise, à	In a flowing style
laisser(z)	To let
lancer	Begin, set in motion
langeur	Listless, lethargic
large	Broad, very slow
le(s)	The
légèrement	Lightly
leicht	Easy, easily

lent	Slow: *See page 9.*
lentement, plus	Holding back
liaison	A tie or slur: ⌒
libre	Free
librement	Freely
lié	Slurred: *Similar to "legato" in Italian.*
limpide	Lucid, clear, transparent
lisse	Smooth, slick
loin	Afar, distant
lourd	Heavy, profound: *Similar to "pesante" in Italian.*
louré	For string players, slightly detached notes played on the string: *See "portato" on page 214.*
lucide	Clear, consistent
luisant	Brilliant, glistening
lumineux	Brilliant, clear
lyrique	Lyrical, emotional

M

mailloche	Percussion stick or mallet
main droite	(*m.d.*) Right hand
main gauche	(*m.g.*) Left hand
mais	But
majestueux	Majestic: *"Maestoso" in Italian.*
majeur	Major tonality

malice	Mischievous, wickedness
marche	March
marqué	Marked, accented
martelé	Short, sharp, heavy accent: *Also called a "heavy wedge." For string players, a short, sharp attack without the bow leaving the string. See page 221.*

méchamment	Viciously, mischievously
méchant	Wicked, nasty
mélancolique	Melancholy, sad, soulful
mélange	Medley
mélodique	Melodic
mélopée	Monotonous, chant
même, de	Similarly: *As in "same tempo."*
menaçant	Menacing, threatening
messe	Mass
mesuré	Measured, in exact time
métre	Measure, beat
mettre; mettez	To put on: *As with a mute.*
milieu	Middle
modèrè	Moderate: *See page 9.*
moëlleux	Soft, but with richness
moins	Less
moins, encore	Still less
moins, le	The least: *As in "le moins possible" (the least possible).*

moins que	Less than
moitié	Half
monotone	Monotonous, without emotion
montant	Increase in dynamic, *cresc.*
moqueur	Mocking, humorous
morceau	A piece, composition
mordant	Sharp, piercing
morne	Dreary, dismal
motif conducteur	A musical motive or theme: *"Leitmotiv" in German.*
mourant, en	Dying away, fading
mourir	Dying away
mouvement	Movement
mouvementé	Bustling, colorful
muet; muette	Silent, mute
murmurer	To murmur, whisper
mystérieux	Mysterious
mystique	Mystical

N

naïf; naïve	Naive, simple
narquois	Mockery, satire
naturel	Natural, normal
naturels, sons	Cancels out the harmonic
ne	Not
ne-pas	To not, do not

nerveux	Nervous, excitable
net	Clear, distinct
niaisiment	Mockingly
noire	Quarter note: ♩
non	No, not
nonchalamment	Casually, with indifference
non vibrez	No vibrato
normale	Normal, ordinary
nostalgique	Sentimental, yearning
nourri, bein	With a full, rich tone, enthusiastic
nouveau, á	New, again
nuancer	With a variety of expression

O

octavin	Piccolo: *Octavin is rarely used in the literature, instead, the Italian word "piccolo" is used in French literature.*
oeuvre	Opus
ondoyant	Wavy, vibrato
opéra bouffe	Comic opera
orageux	Stormy, violent
orgue	Organ
ôter(z)	Remove, take off (as in mute)
ou	Or, or else
ouvert	Open, unstopped

P

paisible	Peaceful, calm
palpitant	Exciting, throbbing
parlé	To speak or talk
partition	A score
pas	Not
pas à pas	Step by step, gradually
pas, au	Stepping, as in a walking pace, *andante*
passionné	Passionate, expressive
pathétique	Moving, with emotion
paume	Palm of the hand
pause	A pause or break
peau	Skin: *Of a drumhead.*
peine, à	Scarcely, hardly
penaud	Sheepish, timid
pendant	During
pénétrant	Piercing, sharp
perdent, en se	To lose oneself, fading away
petite	Small, little
peu	A little
peu à peu	Little by little
phrasé	Phrasing
pieurant	Weeping
pincé(e)	To pinch: *As in "pizzicato."*

piqué	A short, sharp attack: *A form of staccato that uses more of a bouncing attack. The slur indicates one bow direction.*

piquiren	A string term for bouncing the bow: *See "spiccato" on page 216.*
piston	Cornet
plaque	Non-arpeggio: *Indicates the notes of a chord are to be played simultaneously.*
plein	Full, loud
plus	More
plus encore	Even more
plus en plus	More and more
plus, le	The most
plus que	More than
poignant	Deeply moving, emotional
poing	Fist
pointe	Point or tip of the violin bow
pointu	Sharp
pompeux	Stately, dignified
ponctuer	Punctuate, accent
portez	To hold over, sustain, *legato*
posément	Sedately, steadily
pouce	Thumb
pourtant	Yet, even, however

poussé; pousse(z)	Up bow:

précaution, avec	With care
précédent	Preceding, previous
précipité	Rushing ahead, hurrying
précis	Precise, exact, accurate
premiére	First performance
prendre	To take, get
prenez	Take up, pick up, take hold of
près	Near, close
presque	Almost, nearly
pressant, en	Press on, *accel.*
presser(z)	Hurry, go faster, *accel.*
preste	Very fast: *Also means nimble or agile.*
progressivement	Gradually, progressively
prompt, e	Swift
proprement	Neatly, tidy, properly
pultôt, que	Rather, instead
pupitre	Music stand
pur	Pure sound, transparent

Q

quadruple-croche	Sixty-fourth note:
quant	As for
quasi	Almost, nearly

quatre	Four
que	That
quell(e)	Which, what
quelque	Some
quelque chose	Something
quelquefois	Sometimes, occasionally

R

radieux	Dazzling, glorious
radouci	Calming
rage, avec	With fury
ralentir	To slow down, *rit.*
ramenez	To return
ranimer	Lively
rapide	Rapid, fast: *See page 9.*
rapprocher	Pushing ahead
ravissement	Rapturous
récitant	One solo spoken voice
récit; récitatif	To sing or speak out of tempo and rhythm
recite	To recite: *Performed as a spoken part.*
recueilli	Contemplative, meditative
reculant	Slowing down, holding back
renforçant	Reinforcing, *rinforzando*
répétez	To repeat, restate
répétition	Repetition, repeat

reprenez; reprise	Resume, repeat: *Repeating a section of a composition.*

résolu	Determined, resolved
ressonner, faire	Resonating, resounding
ressortir	To bring out, emphasize
restez	To stay, to remain: *For string instruments, this means to stay in the same position while playing a passage. See page 223.*
retardant; retarder	Slowing down
retenir; retenu; retenez	Holding back, *rit.*
retourner	To return, go back
rêve	Dream, dreamy
revenir; revenez	To return
rêveur	Dreamy
ricochet	For string players, throwing the bow on the string in either an up or down motion
rigueur	Strictly in time, rigorous
ronde	Whole note: o
rondement	Briskly
roulade	A roll or flourish from one tone to another
roulement	The drum roll

rouler	To roll: *As in a drum roll.*
rude	Rough, harsh
rythme	Rhythm, beat

S

saccadé	Jerky, erratic motion
sans	Without
sautillè	A fast staccato using all down bows: *The bow lightly rebounds off the string. See page 223.*
sauvage	Savage, wild
scande	To accentuate rhythm and meter
scène	Stage: *As in "sur le scène" (on stage).*
scintillant	Sparkling, brilliant
sèche, sec	Dry, short
selon	According to
sensible	Sensitive
sentiment, avec beaucoup de	With much feeling, emotion
séparé	Separate, divide
septuor	Septet
serein	Quiet, calm, tranquil
serrant, en; serrez	Speed up, moving forward
serré	Tight: *As in a tight tremolo.*
seul(e)	Only, alone

seulement	Solely, exclusively
s'evanouir	Fading away
sifflant	Whistling
siffler	To whistle
signe	Sign: 𝄋 *As in "Del Segno."*
simple	Simple, unpretentious
soigneusement	Carefully, conscientiously
solennel	Solemn, grave, serious
sombre	Gloomy, melancholy
somnolent	Sleepy, drowsy
son	Sound, tone
sonner	To let sound
sonore	Sonorous
sons réels	Sounds as written
sons voilé	Muted, dampened
soudainement	Suddenly, unexpectedly
souffle	Breath, breathing
souffrant	Suffering
soupir	Sigh, also a quarter-note rest
souple	Flexible, yielding, supple
sourd	Dull: *Can also mean to use a mute.*
sourdine	Mute, dampen
soutenu	Sustained, held
strictement	Strictly, purely, exactly
strophe	Verse, stanza
subi; subitement	Suddenly, *subito*

suivre(z)	To follow: *As in "suivez les solo" (follow the solo).*
suppliant	Appealing, imploring
sur	On, upon, over

T

talon, au (du)	For string players to play at the heel or frog of the bow: *See page 224.*
tambour	Drum
tambour de Basque	Tambourine
tempête	Stormy, tempestuous
temps	Beat or time
tendrement	Tenderly, lovingly
tenu	Held, sustained: *Similar to "tenuto" in Italian.*
timbale, une	One timpani
timbales	Timpani, kettledrums
timbre	Sound, tone color
timide	Timidly
tirer vers le haut	To slide upwards
ton	Sound, tone, pitch
touche	Keyboard instrument, fingerboard of a string instrument

touche, sur la	For string players, bowing lightly over the fingerboard: *Producing a flute-like effect. See page 224.*
touché	Touched, emotionally affected
toujours	Always
tous; tout; toute	All, every
traduit; traduction	Arranged, transposed
traîner	To drag, hold back
tranchant	Sharp, incisive
tranquille	Calm, peaceful
tremblement	Tremble, quiver
très	Very
très lié	Well connected, legato
trille	Trill
triolet	Triplet
triple-croche	Thirty-second note: ♪
triste	Mournful, plaintive
triumphant	Triumphant, jubilant, exultant
trois	Three
trompette	Trumpet
trop	Too, too much
trottinant, en	Moving at a steady pace
tumultueux	Violent, commotion
turbulent	Turbulent, boisterous

U

un(e)	A, an, or the number one
uni(s)	In unison, together
uniforme	Evenly spaced, consistent

V

vague	Veiled, subdued
valeur	Time value
vaporeux	Hazy, misty, transparent
variante	Variation
vaut	Is equal to: *As in one note value is equal to another note value.*
véhémente	Intense, passionate
vent	Wind: *As in "comme le vent" (like the wind).*
vibrant	Vibrating, with vibrato
vibrer, laissez	(L.V.) Let ring: *Do not dampen the sound.*
vide	Open string: *See "corda vuota" on page 211.*
vif	Lively, animated: *See page 9.*
vigoureusement	Vigorously, forcefully
viole	Viola
violent	Violent, furious

violon	Violin
violoncelle	Cello
violon solo	Concertmaster: *The first chair musician of the violin section.*
vite	Quickly, fast
voile	Veiled, subdued
voix	Voice
volonté, à	At your pleasure, *ad lib.*
volubile	Fluent, smooth, eloquent
volupté	Full, rich, sensual

Musical Directives – German

A

abbrechen	To stop, cut off
abgemessen	Measured, in strict time
abgesetzt; *abgestossen*	Detached, *staccato*
abklingen	Fading away
ablösen; *abstossen*	To separate the notes in a *staccato* manner
abnehmen	To get softer: *As in "diminuendo."*
abreissen	To tear away (cut off)
Abschlag	A cut off: //
abschwellen	To get softer: *As in "decrescendo."*
absetzen	To take off
Abstrich	Down bow:

abstürzend	Immediately softer: *As in "subito."*
abwechseln	To change, alternate: *A directive for players to alternate between two instruments.*
Achtelnote	Eighth note: ♪
Achtelpause	Eighth rest: ♪
akzentuiert	Accented, marked

alle	All
allein	Alone, only
allmählich	Gradually
Altgeige	Viola
altväterisch	Dignified
am	At the, on the, to the, by the
an	On, by, to, at
anblasen	To blow strongly, to force the tone
Andacht, mit	With reverence
andächtig	Reverently, devoutly
Anfang	Beginning: *As in "da Capo" (from the beginning).*
Anfang Zeitmass	A tempo
angemessen	Comfortable
angenehm	Pleasant, agreeable
ängstlich	Timidly
angstvoll	Anxious
anhalten	To hold out: *Similar to a "fermata."*
Anhang	Coda
anlaufen	To increase in volume: *As in "crescendo."*
Anmerkung	A note or a remark to a musician or conductor
anmutig	Gracefully, charming
anreissen	To rip or tear: *A strong down-bow or pizzicato attack. Same as "gerissen." See page 225.*

Ansatz	The basic approach or embouchure in playing a wind instrument or the proper position for strings
anschlagen	To strike or attack: *The "touch" in piano playing.*
anschwellend	To swell, *crescendo*: ⟨
Anstimmen	Tuning, intonation
Anstrich	A stroke of the bow
anwachsend	To grow: *As in "crescendo."*
Arie	Aria
Arpeggieren	Arpeggio: *See "arpège" on page 58.*
artig	Pleasing, nicely
atemlos	Breathlessly
auch	Also, too
Auf	On, until, open
auf I	For violin to play on the E string
auf II	For violin to play on the A string
auf III	For violin to play on the D string
auf IV	For violin to play on the G string
aufführen	To perform
Aufführung	A performance
aufgebracht	Angry, furious
aufgehängt	Suspended, hanging
aufgeregt	Agitated
aufgeweckt	Bright, animated
aufhalten	To hold back, *ritard*
Auflage	Edition

Auflösen	The natural sign: ♮
Auflösung	A release sign to lower the pedal on the harp of an already-raised string
Aufschlag	Upbeat
Aufschnitt	A "cut" in the score or part: *To omit a section of music.*
aufschwingend	Soaring, with energy
Aufschwung	Momentum, uplift
aufsetzen	To put on
Aufstrich	Up bow for strings:

Auftakt	Upbeat
Auftritt	A scene in an opera
Aufzug	An act in an opera
ausbreiten	To spread out, slowing down
ausdruckslos	Without expression
ausdruckvoll	With expression, *espressivo*
Ausgabe	Edition
ausgeglichen	Evenly, steady, balanced
ausgelassen	With high spirits, exuberant
ausgehalten	Held out, sustained
aushalten	To sustain, hold out
ausholen	To strike
ausschwingen	Dying away
äußerst; äussert	Extremely
Auszug	Arrangement or reduction

B

bebend	Tremolo:

Becken	Cymbals: *See "patti" on page 147.*
bedächtig	Slowly, unhurried
bedeckt	Covered, dampened: *Also, to play the snare drum with the snares in the "off" position.*
bedeuten	Important, significant
bedrohlich	Threatening
befestigen	To fasten or attach
Begeisterung	With enthusiasm
beginnen(d)	To begin, start
begleiten	To accompany
behäbig	Leisurely, comfortable
behaglich	Contented, comfortable
behende	Nimbly
bei	At
beide	Both
beim	At the
beinahe	Nearly, almost

Beisser	A mordent:

beklemmt	Oppressive, anxious
belebend	Lively, animated
belebt	Brisk, *animato*
Belieben, nach	At your discretion
bequem	Comfortable, easily
beruhigend	Calming, slowing down
beschaulich	Reflective, contemplative
beschleunigen	Hasten, quicken
beschwingt	Lively
beseelt	Animated
besinnlich	Thoughtful, attentive
besorgt	Anxious, uneasy
bestimmt	Decisive, firm, prominent
betonen; betont	To accent
Betonung	Accent mark:

Betonung, mit	With emphasis, accented
betrübt	Sadly, sorrowfully
beweglich	Agile
bewegt	Moving, with motion, agitated
bewegter	Moving faster: *As in "più mosso."*

Bindebogen; *Bindungszeichen*	Slur: ⌒
binden	To play in a *legato* manner
Bindung	A tie between two notes:

bis	Until, up to
bisschen, ein	A little
bissig	Vicious, sharp
bittend	Pleading, urging
Blasinstrumente	Wind instruments
Blechinstrumente	Brass instruments
Blechmusik	Brass band
bleiben	To stay, remain
Bogen	The bow for string instruments: *It can also mean a slur or tie.*
Bogenspitze, mit	With the point (tip) of the bow: *See page 225.*
Bogenstrich	The bow stroke
Bratsche(n)	Viola
breit	Broad, slow: *See page 10.*
brummen	To hum: *To produce a tone without words.*
Brummstimme	Humming voices
Bühne	Stage
burlesk	Comic, witty

C

Choralmässig	In the style of a chorale
Concertstück	A concert piece or concerto

D

dämonisch	Devilish, fiendish
dämpfen	To dampen or muffle
Dämpfer	Mute: *As in Mit Dämpfer (with mute) or Dämpfer weg (without mute).*
Dämpfer absetzen	To take off mute
Dämpfer aufsetzen	To put on mute
dasselbe	The same
dehnen	To lengthen, prolong
deklamieren	To recite or perform as a recitative
delikat	Delicate, sensitive
demütig	Humble, unassuming
der; den; die; das	The
derb	Rough, coarse, crude
detonieren	To sing off pitch
deutlich	Clear, distinct
Dirigent	Conductor
Diskordanz	Dissonance

doppel	Double: *See page 10.*
drängend	Pressing forward: *As in "accel."*
dreifach	Triple stop:

Dreitaktig	Three beats to the measure
dringend	Urgent, desperate, pressing
drohend	Threatening, menacing
Druck	Pressure (pressing forward)
duftig	Sweetly, lightly
dumpf	Dull thud or stroke
dünn	Thin, fine, tenuous
durchaus	Absolutely
durchdringen	Driving through, pressing
durchsichtig	Transparent, clear
düster	Gloomy, mournful

E

ebenso	Likewise, similar, just the same
edel	Noble, lofty
eigensinnig	Unyielding, inflexible
eilen; eilig	To hurry, move forward
eilfertig	Hastily, urgently
ein	One, a, an
eindringlich	Urgent, insistent
einfach	Simple, plain

Eingang	Introduction
Einhalt	A pause: '
Einleitung	Introduction
einlenkend	Softening one's tone
einmal	Once more, once again
Einsatz	An accent, attack:

einschlafen	Dying away, *morendo*
Einschnitt	Cut off, *cæsura: //*
ekstatisch	Extreme emotional excitement
elastisch	Flexible
emfindungsvoll	Full of feeling, with emotion
energisch	With energy, vigorous
enthusiastisch	Enthusiastic
entrüstet	Indignant, anger
entschieden	Emphatic, definitive
entschlossen	Determined, without hesitation
entspannen	Relax, easing
entzücken	Delightful, charming
ergeben	With devotion, faithful
ergriffen	Deeply moving, with emotion
erhaben	Noble, with grandeur
erhöhen	To increase the dynamic
erklingen	Ring out
erlöschen(d)	Dying away, *morendo*
ermatten	Growing weak, exhausted

ermunter(n)	Animated, encouraged
ernst	Serious
erregt	Excited, energized
errichten	Established
erschöpft	Exhausted
erschrocken	Terrified, frightened
erschütter(n)	To shake
erst(es)	First
erweitern	To broaden, become slower
erzählen	To narrate, recitative
Erzähler	Narrator
etwas	Somewhat, rather
eventuell	Maybe, possibly

F

Fagott	Bassoon
falsettirend	Falsetto, artificially high-pitched voice
fanatisch	Fanatical, frenzied
Färbung	Tone, sound
Fassung	Version
feierlich	A solemn celebration
Fermate	Fermata: $\frown$
Ferne, in der	In the distance (offstage)
fertig	Quick, nimble
fest(es)	Firm, solid

festlich	Festive
feurig	Fiery, passionate
Fingersatz	Fingering
finster	Dark, gloomy, sinister
Fistelstimme	An artificially high singing voice: *As in "falsetto" in Italian.*
Flatterzunge	Flutter tongue
flehend	Pleading, beseechingly
fließend	Flowing
flimmernd	Glimmering
Flöte	Flute
flott	Brisk, lively
flüchtig	Fleeting, flighty
flüssig	Fluid, flowing, smooth
flüstern(d)	Whispering
fortsetzend	Continuing, resume
fortwährend	Continual, constant
frei	Freely
Freuden, mit	With pleasure
freudig	Joyful, happy
freundlich	Gentle, pleasant
friedlich	Peaceful, quiet
frisch	Brisk, vigorous
frivol	Frivolous, flippant
froh	Joyous, elated
fröhlich	Cheerful, happy
frohlockend	Rejoicing, triumphant

fromm	Religiously, with devotion
Frosch	Frog: *As in "am Frosch" [playing at the 'frog' (nut) end of a bow] for string instruments. See page 227.*
früheres	Earlier
Fuge	Fugue: *A musical form using imitative counterpoint.*
führend	To conduct

G

gallant	Gallant, stately
Galopp	A dance in 2/4 time
Ganze	Whole note: o
gebunden	Tied together: *As in "legato."*
gedämpft	Dampened, muted: *Can also mean "snares off " for snare drum.*
gedeckt	Stopped: *To modify the tone of a French horn by inserting the hand into the bell.*
gedehnt	Slowing, sustaining
gefallen	As you please: *As in "ad lib."*
gefällig	Pleasing, graceful
gefaßt	Calm, composed
Gefühl, mit	With feeling
gefühlvoll	Full of feeling, expressively
gehalten	Sustained, to hold
gehaucht	To breathe or sigh: *Softly and lightly.*
geheimnisvoll	Mysteriously

gehend	To go or move: *As in "andante." See page 10.*
Geige	Violin
gelassen	Calmly, with composure
geläufig	Fluently, smooth
gelöst	Detached
gemächlich	In a leisurely manner: *As in "andante."*
gemäßigt	Moderately
gemessen	Measured, steady tempo
gemischt	Mixed: *As in "gemischte stimmen" (mixed voices).*
gemütlich	In a leisurely manner
gering	Small
gerissen	To rip or tear: *A strong down-bow attack for string players. See page 227.*
gerührt	Stirred, moved: *With emotion.*
gesangvoll	Lyrical, in a singing manner
geschäftig	Bustling, energetic
geschlagen	To hit or strike
geschleift	Looped or slurred: *As in "legato."*
geschmackvoll	Tastefully
geschmeidig	Flexible, supple
geschwind	Quickly, swiftly
gespannt	Tense, strained
gesprochen	Spoken
gesteigert	Increasing in volume, *cresc.*
gestopft	Stopped: *To modify the tone of a French horn by inserting the hand into the bell.*

gestossen	Disconnected, *staccato*
gestrichen	Smooth and connected: *As in "legato."*
gesummt	Humming
gesungen	Sung
geteilt	Divided, *divisi*
getragen	Solemn, sustained
gewichtig	Important
gewissen	Certain, particular: *As in "mit einem gewissen Schwung" (with a certain swing).*
gewöhnlich	Ordinary, common
geworfen	Bouncing the bow rapidly on string instruments: *See page 228.*
glänzend	Brilliant, dazzling
glashart	Hard as glass, clear
gleich	Same, identical
gleichförmig	Equal, uniform
gleichgültig	Indifferent, careless
gleichmässig	Even, regular
gleichzeitig	Non-arpeggio: *This indicates the notes of a chord are to be played simultaneously.*
gleitend	Smoothly, gliding
glitzernd	Glittering, sparkling
Glocke	Chimes, large bell
Glockenspiel	Orchestra bells
glühend	Glowing, fervent
Griffbrett, am	Playing with the bow over the fingerboard of string instruments: *See page 229.*

grotesk	Grotesque, bizarre
Grundeinheit	Basic meter
Grundtempo	Basic tempo
gut	Good

H

H	The note "B natural" in music
Halbe	Half note: ♩
halten	To hold, sustain
Haltung	Fermata, pause: ⌒
hämmern	To hammer, pound
hart	Hard, tough, severe
Härte	Harshness, relentlessness
hastig	Hastily, abrupt
Hauch, wie ein	Like a breath or touch: *Very lightly.*
Hauptstimme	Principal voice or theme
Hauptzeitmass	Main tempo
heftig	Violent, intense
heftigkeit, mit	Violence, fierceness
heilig	Holy, sacredly
heimlich	Secretly, mysterious
heiter	Cheerful, jovial: *Similar to "scherzando" in Italian.*
heldenhaft	Heroically
hell	Bright, clear
heraus	Out

herausheben	Marked, accented
heraustimmen	To retune: *See page 229.*
herrisch	Masterfully, authoritatively
Herunterstreich	Down bow:

hervor	Marked, to bring out
hervorbrechend	Erupting
hervorgehoben	Emphasized, accented
hervorheben	To bring out
hervortretend	Indicating the principal voice:

Ein Heldenleben - Richard Strauss

herzig	Tenderly, sweetly
herzlich	With warmth, affection
Hinaufstreich	Up bow:

hinaufziehen	To slide upwards
Hingebung, mit	With devotion, dedication
hinhaltend	Delaying, holding back

hinsterbend	Fading away, *morendo*
hinströmend	Flowing
hoch; höchster	High, highest
Höhepunkt	Climax
höhnisch	Scornful, taunting
Holz	Wood
Holz, das	The woodwind section of an orchestra
hörbar	Audible
hüpfend	Skipping, hopping
hurtig	Nimble, agile, lively
huschend	Hurrying, darting, moving quickly
hymnenartig	Hymn like

I

im; ins	In the: *As in "im tempo" (in the tempo).*
immer	Always
inbrünstig	With warmth of feeling, fervently
in der Ferne	In the distance, offstage
innig	Sincere, intimate
inniglich	With deep emotion
inständig	Urgently
intensiv	Intensively, vigorously

J

jauchzend	Cheering, joyous
jede(r)	Every, each
jedesmal	Every time, each time
jedoch	However, yet
jubelnd	Jubilantly, cheering
jünglingshaft	Youthful

K

Kadenz	Cadenza, cadence
kadenzartig	Like a cadenza
kaprizös	Capriciously, fanciful
kaum	Hardly, scarcely
keck	Bold, confident
Keckheit, mit	With confidence
kein(e)	No, none
kindlich	Childlike
Kirchenmusik	Church music
klagend	Lament, mournfully
kläglich	Pitiful, mournful
Klang	A resonating sound
Klangfarbe	Tone color: *Similar to "timbre" in French.*
klangvoll	Melodious, sonorous

klar	Clear, articulate
Klarinette	Clarinet
Klavier	Piano: *The instrument not the dynamic.*
klein(e)	Small, little
klingen lassen	Let sound, let ring
klingt octave höher	Sounds one octave higher
klingt wie notiert	Sounds as written
kokett	Flirtatious, coquettish
Kontrabass	Double bass
Kontrafagott	Contrabassoon
Konzerstück	Concert piece: *Generally referring to a concerto for soloist and orchestra.*
Kornett	Cornet
kosend	Caressingly
Kraftentfaltung	Unveiling of strength
kräftig	Forcefully, vigorously
kreischend	Screechy, shrilling
Kreuz	The sharp sign: ♯
kriegerisch	Warlike, military
kühn	Boldly
kurz	Short
kurzatmig	Dull

L

lang(e)	Long
langsam	Slow: *Similar to "Lento" in Italian. See page 10.*
lassen	To let, allow
lässig	Casually, airy
lastend	Weighty, oppressive
launig; launisch	Capricious, moody
laut	Loudly, rowdy
lauter werdend	Becoming louder, *cresc.*
lebendig	Lively, feisty
lebhaft	Lively, animated: *See page 10.*
leibkosend	Caressingly
leichtfertig	Rash, frivolous
leichtlich	Lightly, easily
leidenschaftlich	Passionate
leidvoll	Sorrowful, full of grief
Leiern	Sound of wind, droning
leigen lassen	To hold or keep down
leise	Quietly, softly, gentle
leiser werdend	Becoming softer, *decresc.*
Leitmotiv	A musical motive or theme
letzt	Last
liebeglühend	Burning with love
liebenswürdig	Pleasing

lieblich	Lovely, charming
Lied	Song
linke Hand	Left hand
lispelnd	With a lisp
locker	Loose, relaxed
losbrechen	Breaking out, bursting
luftig	Airy
Luftpause	A breath mark, a short pause: '
lustig	Jolly, merrily
lyrisch	Lyrical, melodic

M

mächtig	Powerful, loud
majestätisch	Majestic, *maestoso*
Mal	Time: *As in "erste Mal" (first time).*
Manieren	Ornaments or grace notes
märchenhaft	Fairytale, magical
markiert	Accented, marked: *Similar to "marcato" in Italian.*
markig	Brief, to the point
Marsch	March
massig	Massive
mäßig	Moderate, reserved: *See page 10.*
mehr	More
mehrere	Many, several
melancholisch	Melancholy, depressing

melodie	Melody
merklich	Noticeably
Messe	Mass
mit	With
möglich	Possible: *As in "so rasch wie möglich" (as fast as possible).*
moll	Minor tonality
monoton	Monotonous, without emotion
müde	Tired, weary
munter	Lively, animated
murmelnd	Whispered
mutig	Courageous, boldly
mystisch	Mystical

N

nach	After
nach und nach	Little by little, gradually
nachdenklich	Thoughtful, reflective
Nachdruck, mit	With emphasis
nachgebend	To give way, yield
nachlassen	Become slower, holding back
nachlässig	Carelessly
Nachschlag	The note or notes following a trill:

nächsten	Near, nearest
nächtlich	Nocturnal, dark, gloomy
näherkommend	Nearing, approaching
näseln	A nasal tone
natürlich	Natural style: *Without ornaments, mutes, etc.*
necktisch	Teasing, playful
nervös	Nervous, irritated
neu	New
nicht	Not
nichts	Nothing
Niederschlag	Downbeat
nimm	Take
noch	Still, rather
noch einmal	Once more, once again
normal	Normal, standard
nur	Only, just

O

oben	Above
oder	Or
offen	Open: *Unstopped for French horn.*
ohne	Without
Oktavflöte	Piccolo
Orgel	Organ

P

Paar	Pair
Palltriller	An inverted mordent:

Partitur	Full score
pathetisch	Emotional, with feeling
Pauken	Timpani
Pause	A break or pause: **'**
pedantisch	Pedantic, unemotional
peitschen	To swish, lash
pendelnd	Swinging: *As in the motion of a pendulum.*
pfeifen	To whistle
pfeifig	Whistling
pfiffig	Precise, accurate
phantastisch	Fantastic, fanciful
phrasiert	Phrasing
Piston	Cornet
plötzlich	Suddenly, *subito*
pomp; pomphaft	Grandiose, stately
pompös	Excessive, pretentious
Posaune	Trombone
possierlich	Cute, sweetly
prächtig	Magnificent, splendid

prachtvoll	Gorgeously, magnificent
prononciert	Pronounced
prunkvoll	Pompous, dignified
Pultweise geteilt	Divide part by stand, *divisi*

Q

Quadrat	The natural sign: ♮

R

Rand, am	On the edge
rasch	Quickly, fast
rasend	Madly, rage
raserei, mit	With fury
rauh	Rough, harshly
rauschend	Whispering, murmuring
recht	Right, absolutely: *As in "recht gemessen" (absolutely measured).*
rechte Hand	Right hand
regelmässig	Regular, uniform
rezitativ	To sing or speak out of tempo and rhythm
rezitieren	To recite
rhythmistiert	Rhythmical
ritterlich	Chivalrous
robust	Strong, vigorous

roh	Crude, rough
rückkehrend	Returning
Rücksicht, ohne	Regardless, without consideration
rücksichtslos	Reckless, ruthless
ruhelos	Restless
ruhevoll	Calm, peaceful
ruhig	Quiet, calm, peaceful
ruhiger	Calmer, more quiet
Rührung	Emotion

S

Saite	String: *Of a violin, viola, etc.*
sanft	Gentle, soft
sanftmütig	Meekly
satt; sattem	Full: *As in "mit sattem Gefühl" (with full emotion).*
Satz	Movement of a symphony
schalkhaft	Mischievously
Schallrichter, auf	Bells up: *An instruction for the French horn to lift the bell of their instrument above the music stand while playing.*
scharf	Sharp, piercing
scharrend	Scraping, a grating sound
schattenhaft	Shadowy, in the background
schaudernd	Shuttering, shivering
schaurig	Ghastly, horrible

schelmisch	Mischievous
scherzhaft	Humorous, playful
schlag	To strike
Schlagwerk	Percussion section
schleichend	Creeping, sneaking
schleppen	To drag, *rit.*
schlicht	Simple, plain
schluchzend	Sobbing
Schlüssel; Schluß	Musical clef:

schmachtend	Languishingly, longing
schmeichelnd	Caressing, flattering
schmelzend	Dying away
schmerzlich	Painfully, sorrowfully
schmetternd	For French horn players to play with a "brassy" tone: *Produced with the hand inserted into the bell (stopped) and blowing hard.*
Schmiß, mit	With enthusiasm, passion
schnarrend	Rattle or buzzing sound
schneidend	Incisively, cutting, sharp
schnell	Fast, quick: *See page 10.*
schneller	Faster
schnippisch	Sharp, cracking sound
schon	Already
schön	Beautiful
schreitend	Moving ahead

Schritt	Pace, tempo
schrittmässig	At a moderate pace
schroff	Brusque, abrupt
schüchtern	Tentatively
schwach	Weak, faint
schwärmerisch	Ecstatic, emotional
schwebend	Floating, soaring
schwebungsfrei	Without beats or pulse: *Non mesura.*
Schweigen	Silence, to be silent
Schweigezeichen	The silent sign, **G.P.**: *Grand Pause.*
schwelgend	Sensual, luxurious
schwellen	Swelling, to get louder
schwer	Heavy, ponderous
schwerfällig	Heavy, ponderously, clumsy
schwermütig	Melancholy
schwindend	Fading, dying away
Schwung, mit	With momentum
schwungvoll	Vigorous, spirited
Sechzehntel	Sixteenth note: ♪
Seele	Soul, spirit, with feeling: *Also the "sound post" of a string instrument.*
seelenvoll	Soulfully
Sehnsucht	Longing, yearning
sehr	Very
selbe	Same
selig	Blissful, blessed
Seufzer	Heartfelt, sighing

sieghaft	Victorious
silbern	Silvery, clear bell-like tone
singend	Singing, *cantabile*
so	As, so
sofort	At once, immediately, *subito*
sogar	Actually
sordun	Muffled, muted
sorglos	Careless, carefree
spaßhaft	Jokingly, *scherzando*
spielen	To play
spielend	Playfully
spielenrein	To play in tune
spielenunrein	To play out of tune
spielen zu hoch	To play sharp
spielen zu tief	To play flat
Spieler	Player
Spitze	Point (tip) of the bow
spitzig	Pointed, sharp
Sprechstimme	Spoken song, speech song: *Singers approximate pitch while speaking the rhythms.*
springend	For string players, bouncing the bow against the strings: *See page 231.*
stammelnd	Babbling, stammering
Stange	Stick (wood) of the bow: *Similar to "col legno." See page 231.*
stark	Strong, powerful
starr	Rigid, stiff, inflexible

Steg, am	For string players to play near the bridge: *See page 231.*
steigern(d)	Increasing in tempo or dynamic
sterbend	Dying away, *morendo*
stetig	Continuous, steadily
stets	Always
Stil	Style
still	Quiet, softly
Stimme	Voice
Stimmung	Mood, atmosphere
stockend	Hesitating, holding back
stoltz	Glorious, joyful
straff	Firm, tight, steady
strahlend	Brilliant, radiant
Streich; Strich	Stroke: *As in "breiter Strich" (broader stroke)* for string players.
streicheln	To stroke: *As in "breit streicheln" (with broad strokes).*
Streicher	The string section, string players
streng	Strict, severe: *As in "streng im Takt" (strictly in time).*
strömend	Flowing
Strophen	Verses
Stück	A musical work
Stufe	Pitch or scale step
stumm	Silent
stürmisch	Stormy, tempestuous
süß	Sweetly

T

Takt, im	In strict time
Takt, ohne	In free time and rhythm, *rubato*
Takt(e)	A measure (bar): *A beat of time.*
Takteineilung, ohne	Without bar lines: *Non-mesura.*
Tanz	Dance
Teil	Part, section
teilen	To divide: *See "divisi" on page 211.*
Tempover-änderung	Change of tempo
tief	Deep, profound, low in pitch
Ton	A tone, sound, pitch
Tonart	Key signature, tonality
Tonfall	Intonation
Tonkünstler	Composer
Tonleiter	A musical scale
tonlos	Soundless, toneless
Tonsatz	A composition
tonvoll	Tuneful, melodious
träge	Slow: *Similar to "langsam."*
Trauer, mit	With sorrow or grief
Trauermusik	Funeral music
trauig	Sad, sorrowful
Traum	Dream

Triller	Trill
träumerisch	Dreamy
treibend	Hurrying, moving ahead
triumphierend	Triumphantly, exultant
trocken	Dry, impassive
Trommel	Drum
Trompete	Trumpet
trüb(e)	Dull, gloomy

U

üben	To practice
über	Over, above
überall	Everywhere
übergehen	Ignore, leave out
überlegen	Deliberate, predominant
überleiten	To segue, transition
übermäßig	Exuberant, excessive
übermütig	High spirited
überschwenglich	Exuberantly, gushing forth
überströmend	Exuberant, overflowing
ubertrieben	Exaggerated
Überzeugung, mit	With conviction
übrigen, die	The remaining (players)
um	Around, at, for, about
unbetont	Unaccented
und	And

ungduldig	Impatiently
ungebunden	Freely
ungefähr	Approximately, roughly
ungehemmt	Uninhibited
ungemein	Exceptionally, exceedingly
ungestüm	Turbulence, tumultuous
unhörbar	Inaudible
unmerklich	Imperceptible
unmitig	To show displeasure
unregelmäßig	Irregular, erratic
unrhytmisch	Irregular, uneven
unruhig	Anxious, restless
unschuldig	Innocently
unstimmen	To retune
unten	Down, below, under
unter	Under
Unterbrechung, ohne	Without a break or pause
üppig	Exuberant, elaborate
ursprünglich	Original

V

Ventil	Valve horn
verbreiten	Spreading, becoming slower
verdichten	To condense or compress, *accel.*
vergnügt	Cheerfully

verhallend	Dying away
verlierend	Fading away
verlöschen	Fading away
verschleiert	Muffled, muted
verschwindend	Vanishing, dying away
versetzen	To transpose
Versetzung	Transposition
Versetzungs- *zeichen*	Accidental
versonnen	Dreamy, lost in thought
verstärken	To boost or enhance, get louder
verstimmt	Out of tune
verträumt	Dreamy
verweilend	Delay, *ritenuto*
Verzierungen	Ornaments or embellishments: *See* *"acciaccatura" and "appoggiatura" in* *Italian on pages 12 and 15.*
verzögert	Delayed, getting slower
verzückt	Ecstatic, emotional
verzweifelt	Desponded, hopeless, anguish
viel	Much
vielstimmig	Polyphonic
vier	Four
Viertel	Quarter note: ♩
Vierteln, in	In quarters (conduct in four)
Vierundsech- *zigsel*	Sixty-fourth note: ♪

Violoncello	Cello
voll	Full
vollständig	Completely, fullest
volltönend	Sonorous, resonant, with a full tone
vom	From, from the
von	Of, about, from
voran	Preceding, before
vorangehen	Going ahead, continuing
vorbereiten	To prepare for
Vorhang	Stage curtain
vorher	Before, previously
vorigen	Preceding, previous
Vorschlag	A grace note with a distinct harmonic application (different from an ornament): *This grace note is played on the beat and takes ½ of the following note value.*

Vorspeil	Prelude, introduction, overture
Vortragzeichen	Expression mark
vorwärts	Forward, moving ahead, *più mosso*

W

wachsend	Growing louder, *crescendo*
Waldhorn	The French horn
Walzer	Waltz
Wärme, mit	With warmth
wechselnd	Changing, alternative
weg	Away, off
Weh	Pain, grief, distressed
wehmütig	Wistfully, with sadness or melancholy
weich	Soft, tender, gentle
weichflüssig	Flowing smoothly
weihevoll	Solemnly, religiously
weinend	Weeping
weinerlich	Mournful, tearfully
weiter	Resume, proceed
weiterklingen	Continuing to sound, sustain
wenig ein	A little: As in *"so wenig wie möglich"* (*as little as possible*).
weniger	Less
werdend	Becoming
wesentlich	Essential, vital
wie	As, how, like
wieder	Again
wiegend	Swaying, lullaby

wie oben	As above
wie zuvor	As before
wild	Wild, passionate
womöglich	If possible
wuchtig	Weighty, heavy, with strong emphasis
wuchtiger, etwas	Somewhat massive
würdig	Dignified, stately
wütend	Raging, furiously

Z

zaghaft	Timid, weak
zart	Delicate, tender, soft, *dolce*
zärtlich	Tenderly, lovingly
Zäsur	A short break or pause: //
zeistimmig	For two voices, or in two parts
Zeit	Time, tempo
Zeitmass	Tempo
Ziegeunermusik	Gypsy music
ziehen	To draw out
ziemlich	Rather, somewhat
zierlich	Delicately, gracefully
zitternd	Trembling, shaking
zögernd	Hesitating, holding back
zornig	Angrily
zu	To

zufrieden	Contented, peaceful
zügig	Brisk, quick, rapid
zuletzt	At last, last of all
zum	To the
zunehmend	Increasing, *crescendo*
Zungenschlag	Tonguing
zurückgehend	Returning, going back
zurückhaltend	Holding back, *ritardando*
zurücknehmen	To take back, withdraw
zurücktreten	To recede, getting softer
zusammen	Together, altogether
zuvor	Before
zwanglos	Free and easy, *ad lib.*
zwei	Two
zweite	Second
zweihändig	For two hands
Zweitaktig	Two beats in the measure
zweitelig	Two part
Zweiund- *dreisigstel*	Thirty-second note: ♪
zwischen	Between, among
Zwischensatz	Episode
Zwischenspiel	Interlude, intermezzo

Musical Phrases – German

Accel. (It.) ohne Rüchsicht auf den Takt.
Speed up without regard to the tempo.

Alle Streicher mit furchtbarer Gewalt.
All strings with terrifying power.

Allmählich bewegter, ins Tempo I übergehen.
Gradually moving faster, ignore Tempo I.

Allmählich sich beruhigend.
Gradually slowing down.

Allmählich und stetig drängend.
Gradually and steadily pressing forward.

Allmählich zum nächsten Tempo steigern.
Gradually increasing to the next tempo.

Anmerkung für den Dirigenten.
A note for the conductor.

Beinahe doppelt so schnell.
Nearly twice as fast.

Dasselbe Zeitmass.
The same tempo.

Etwas breiter werden.
Becoming somewhat broader.

Etwas drängend.
Somewhat pressing forward.

Etwas mässiger, aber immer noch sehr lebhaft.
Somewhat moderately, but always still very lively.

Etwas ruhiger, aber immer noch bewegt.
Somewhat peaceful, but always still moving
forward.

Etwas zurückhalten.
Somewhat holding back.

*Fest und bestimmt beginnend, denn allmählich
wieder etwas lebhafter.*
Festive and decisive as in the beginning; then, again,
gradually somewhat lively.

Holzinstrumente sehr hervortretend.
The woodwinds should predominate.

Im errichten Tempo weiter.
Continue in the established tempo.

Im Tempo, mit lebhaftem Schwung.
In tempo, with a lively spirit.

Im Tempo nachgeben.
In a slower tempo.

Im Tempo nachlassen.
In a relaxed tempo.

Immer bewegen.
Always moving forward.

Immer noch etwas vorwärts.
Still somewhat moving forward.

Immer noch mehr zurückhalten.
Always still more holding back.

Immer vorwärts drängend.
Always pressing forward.

In gemessenem Schritt.
At a measured pace (tempo).

In ruhig fliessender Bewegung.
In a calm flowing motion.

Kräftig, aber etwas gemessen.
Forcefully, but somewhat dignified.

Mit Aufschwung, aber nicht eilen.
With momentum, but do not rush.

Mit durchaus ernstem und feierlichen Ausdruck.
With absolutely serious and solemn expression.

Mit einem Mal etwas wuchtiger.
All at once somewhat forceful.

Mit grossem Schwung und Begeisterung.
With great spirit and enthusiasm.

Mit höchster Kraftentfaltung.
With maximum strength.

Morendo (It.) bis zum Schluss.
Dying away until the end.

Nicht eilen.
Do not rush.

Nicht schleppen. (Etwas flüssiger als zu Angang.)
Do not drag. (Somewhat fluid as in the beginning.)

Nicht zurückhalten.
Do not hold back.

Nie eilen.
Never rush.

Noch bewegter, sehr leidenschaftlich.
Still moving forward, very passionate.

Noch etwas langsamer.
Still somewhat slower.

Plötzlich wieder bedeutend langsamer.
Again, suddenly significantly slower.

Plötzlich wieder ruhig und sehr gefühlvoll.
Again, suddenly peaceful and very full of expression.

Schon ziemlich lebhaft.
Already rather lively.

Schwebend, aber ziemlich ruhig.
Soaring, but rather calm.

Sehr bewegt und leidenschaftlich.
Very moving and passionate.

Sehr feierlich, aber schlicht.
Very solemn, but simple.

Sehr gemächlich.
Very much in a leisurely manner.

Sehr getragen und gesangvoll.
Very solemn and in a singing manner.

Sehr langsam und gedehnt.
Very slow and sustained.

Sehr langsam beginnend.
Start very slow.

Sehr mäßig und zurückhalten.
Very moderate and holding back.

Sehr scharf rhythmistiert.
Very sharp rhythm.

Überall schnell abdämpfen.
Quickly dampen everywhere.

Ummerklich etwas einhalten.
Keep rather imperceptible.

Von hier ab fest im Zeitmass.
From here on, the tempo is firm.

*Von hier, allmählich und unmerklich zu Tempo I
zurückhalten.*
From here, gradually and noticeably hold back to
Tempo I.

Wie zu Anfang.
Like the beginning.

Wieder ins Tempo I zurückhalten.
Again, holding back as in Tempo I.

Wieder lebafter, Fest und energisch.
Again, lightly, festive and energetic.

Weider unmerklich zurühalten.
Again imperceptibly holding back.

Percussion Instruments and Terms

Italian

A

a due (a2)	When used on cymbal parts, this refers to two cymbals (crash cymbals)
a una pelle	A single head
acciaio	Steel: *A metal beater or a triangle beater.*
acciarino	Triangle
agitare	To shake or rub
albero de sonagli	Bell tree
allentare	To slacken or loosen
altezza	High pitched
alto	High
arenaiuolo	Maracas
armonica de vetro	A glass harmonica or seraphim: *Wine glasses that are filled with water. A finger is used to rub along the rims to produce a sound.*

B

bacchetta	A drum stick or mallet
bacchetta de canna/bambù	Cane or rattan sticks
bacchetta di ferro	Metal beater: *Triangle beater.*
bacchetta di gran cassa	Bass drum mallet: *Medium to large, felt-covered mallets ranging from soft to hard.*
bachetta di legno	Any wooden stick: *Including snare drum sticks or the wood end of timpani mallets.*
bacchetta di mòlle	Soft-headed mallet
bacchetta di pèlle	Leather-covered mallets
bacchetta di spugna	Sponge-headed mallets: *Refers to a soft mallet. Percussionists use a variety of cord, yarn, or felt-covered mallets instead of a sponge head.*
bacchetta di tamburo	Snare drum stick
bacchetta di triangolo	Triangle beater, metal beater
bambagia	A mallet with a soft cotton or wool covering
bamboo Brasiliano	Brazilian scraper
bambù	Bamboo: *Used for making mallet handles — also called "rattan."*

bambù sospeso	Bamboo wind chimes
barile di legno	A wooden barrel: *Also called a "barrel drum." A two-headed drum, where the center of the shell is larger than the ends and played in a horizontal position with the hands which produce two different tones.*
barile di sake	Sake barrel: *A wooden barrel woven from natural fibers and played with round wooden sticks.*
battere	To hit, beat, or strike
batteria	Percussion section
battuto	Hammered, beaten
batuto cola mano	To play with the hands
bicchieri di vetro	Tuned glasses: *Wine glasses that are filled with water. A finger is used to rub along the rims to produce a sound.*
blòcchi di Cinese	Chinese temple blocks: *Usually found in a set of five blocks, pitched from low to high.*
blòcco di legno	Wood block
blòcco di metallo	Metal block: *Can also include an anvil or cowbell.*
bonghi	Bongo drums: *Always found in a set of two drums.*
bordo	Side or edge
bubbolo	Jingles or sleigh bells
buttibu	A friction or string drum: *Also called a "cuíca" or "Brazilian friction drum."*

C

caccavella	Friction drum: *See "buttibu" on page 136.*
campana	Chimes, large bell
campanaccio	Cow bell
campana d'allarme	Alarm bell
campana da preghiera	Prayer bells
campana di legno	Temple blocks
campana grave	A low-pitched church bell
campana in lastra di metallo	Bell plate: *Various sizes of metal plates, usually struck with a metal hammer or a large brass mallet.*
campana tubolare	Tubular bells, chimes:

Sounds as written.

campanelle	A small bell
campanelle di vacca	Cow bell

campanelli	Orchestra bells: *"Glockenspiel" in German.*

Sounds two octaves higher than written.

campanelli a tastiera	Keyboard orchestra bells
campanello	A small bell: *Sometimes described as a doorbell or hand bell.*
cannone	A cannon or large gun
cariglione	Carillon bells: *A set of large bells operated by a manual or electronic keyboard. Can be substituted with a set of chimes.*
carta sabbiata	Sandpaper blocks
carta vetrata	Sandpaper blocks
cassa	Drum
cassa chiara	Snare drum
cassa di legno	Wood block
cassa di metallo	Metal block: *Can be an anvil, cowbell, or bell plate.*
cassa grande	Bass drum
cassa rullante	Tenor drum: *The tenor drum is played with snares "off." A tenor drum with snares "on" is called a field drum or parade drum.*

castagnetta(e)	Castanets: *Percussionists use handle castanets to reproduce the authentic sound of Spanish "Flamenco" castanets. For a more contemporary sound, use machine castanets.*
castagnette di fèrro; castagnette di metallo	Metal castanets: *Mounted finger cymbals.*
catena	Iron chains
catuba	Bass drum: *This word is rarely found in the literature.*
cencerro	(*L.Amer.*) Cowbell
ceppi cinese	Temple blocks
ceppi di carta vetrata	Sandpaper blocks
cerchio	The counter hoop or rim of a drum head: *The hoop that tightens and loosens the drum head.*
cerchio della pèlle	The flesh hoop: *The hoop attached to the drum head.*
chocallo	(*L. Amer.*) Metal tube shaker
cimbali	Cymbals
cimbali antichi	Antique cymbals: *Tuned metal discs chromatically mounted on a stand. The range is two octaves:*

Sounds two octaves higher than written.

139

cimbalini	Antique cymbals: *May also refer to "finger cymbals."*
cinelli	Cymbals: *A generic word for cymbals — it does not specify "crash" or "suspended."*
cinelli dito	Finger cymbals
clacson	Klaxon horn, taxi horn: *In George Gershwin's* American in Paris, *he writes for four taxi horns pitched in A, B, C, and D.*
colla mano	With the hands
col mazza	With a large mallet
col police	With the thumb
con còrda	With snares: *This refers to playing the snare drum with the snares tightly attached to the bottom head.*
con sordina	With mute: *For bass drum or timpani, it means dampening the head with a cloth. For snare drum, it generally refers to releasing the snares to obtain the sound of a tom-tom.*
coperto(i)	Covered, muted: *It can also refer to releasing the snares on the snare drum.*
còrda; còrdes	Snares: *Refers to the wire, gut, or cable snares attached to the bottom head of a drum.*
corda di minugia	Cat gut, gut snares
crotali	Crotales: *See "cimbali antichi" on page 139.*
cuculo	Cuckoo bird call
cuíca	A Brazilian friction drum
cupola	Cup or dome of a cymbal

D

darabukke
Arabian hand drum: *A single-headed, goblet-shaped hand drum made out of clay or metal with a skin head and tightened by rope or tension rods. It originates from the Middle East and North Africa and is played by holding it under the arm and striking it with fingers and hands.*

diavolo di bosco
Pasteboard rattle: *A metal or wood shell with a single head. A gut string is attached through a hole in the center of the head and vibrated by whirling it in the air against a grooved piece of wood.*

dito
Finger

dura
Hard

E

effètto di piòggia
Rain machine: *A large closed tube with screen wire filled with small pebbles. When rotated, it produces the sound of rain.*

eolifono
Wind machine: *A very large cylinder rotated around heavy canvas by means of a handle that produces the sound of wind.*

escobeta
Wire brushes

F

feltro	Felt
fèrro	Metal
fèrro di triangolo	Triangle beater (metal)
fischierèlla; fischi d'uccelli	Bird whistle
fischietto	Whistle
fischietto a pallina	Police whistle
fischio	Boat or train whistle
fischio sirèna	Mouth siren
fissato	Fixed or attached to
flagèllo	Slapstick, whip
flauto a culisse	Slide whistle
flessatono	Flexatone: *A thin strip of steel attached to a handle with two hard beaters. The player gently shakes the handle, allowing the two beaters to strike the surface of the metal strip. By bending the steel strip with pressure from the thumb, the pitch can be raised or lowered.*
foglie di rame	Metal wind chimes
foglio di metallo	Thunder sheet: *A large thin piece of sheet metal suspended from a frame. When shaken, it makes the sound of thunder.*
fregare	To rub

frullo	Friction drum: *This includes the "cuíca" and "lion's roar."*
frusta	Slapstick, whip
fusto	The shell of a drum

G

ginòcchio	Knee
glissando colla pedale	To make a glissando on the timpani by quickly pressing the pedal: *Glissandi on the timpani are most effective from low to high; however, in slow tempi, they can also be played from high to low.*
gli uccelli	Bird whistle
gomma	Gum or rubber for heads of mallets
gong giapponese; gong giavanese	Japanese nipple or button gong
gracidio di anitra	Duck call
gran cassa	Bass drum
gran cassa a una pèlle	Single-headed bass drum or gong drum
gran tamburo	Bass drum
gran tamburo vecchio	A tenor drum: *With a long shell similar to the "tambourin de provençal" in French. See page 177.*
gregge	Cow bell

guiro	Guiro: *A hollowed-out gourd with notches on the upper body and scraped with a stick.*
guitcharo	(*L.Amer.*) Guiro, gourd scraper

I

idiofono a rasch-iamento; idio-fono raspado	See "guiro" above
incudine	Anvil: *A metal block with a high and low pitch.*
instrumento d'acciaio	Orchestra bells: *See "Glockenspiel" on page 189.*

L

lana	Wool: *A very soft covering for mallets.*
lasciare le cordes	Snares off
lasciar vibrar	(L.V.) Let vibrate: *Do not muffle the sound.*
lastra del tuono; lastra de latta; lastra di metallo	Thunder sheet: *See "foglio di metallo."*
lastra(o) di sasso	Stone disks: *A keyboard instrument made from stone disks. Also known as a "lithophone."*
legnetti	Claves

legni di rumba	Claves
legno	Wood: *Usually refers to wood sticks (snare drum sticks) or the wood end of mallets. Can also refer to a wood block.*
legno frullante	Bull roarer: *A thin piece of wood attached to a string and whirled in the air.*
lero lero	Guiro scraper
litofono	Lithophone: *See "lastra di sasso" on page 144.*

M

macchina à tonnerre; macchina di tuono	Thunder sheet: *See "foglio di metallo" on page 142.*
macchina dal (a) vento; machine à vent	Wind machine: *See "eolifono" on page 141.*
macchina da scrivere; machine à écrire	Typewriter
manico	Handle
maraca di metallo	Metal maraca
marache	Maracas
margine	Edge, rim

marimbafono	Marimba: *Can range from four to five octaves:*

martello	Hammer
mascèlla d'asino	Jawbone of an ass: *The lower jawbone of a mule or donkey. When struck, the teeth rattle. The Spanish name is "quijada" and the modern version is called a "vibraslap."*
membrane	Drum head
mòlle	Soft

N

nacchera	Castanets
nacchera clindrica	Wood blocks
naruco	Wooden wind chimes
noce di cocco	Coconut shells: *Used for making the sound of horse's hooves.*

O

òrgano di legno	Xylophone: *See "xilofono."*
orlo	Edge, rim: *Edge of the drum head or the rim of the drum.*
ottone	Brass: *Refers to brass mallets.*

146

P

pedale apèrto	Open hi-hat pedal
pedale chuiso	Closed hi-hat pedal
pèlle battende	Batter head: *The top head of a drum.*
pèlle cordiera	Snare head: *The bottom head of a drum.*
percòssa	A percussive stroke
percuotere	To strike or hit
percussione	Percussion
piatti	Cymbals: *A generic term that does not specify whether to play on crash or suspended cymbals.*
piatti a due (a2)	Crash cymbals
piatti antichi	Antique cymbals: *See "cimbali antichi" on page 139.*
piatti a pedale	Hi-hat cymbals
piatti sospeso	Suspended cymbal
piatto	One cymbal, a suspended cymbal
piatto cinesi	Chinese suspended cymbal
piatto fissato	Suspended cymbal
piatto susposo	Suspended cymbal
piccolo cassa	A small, high pitched snare drum
piccolo timpani	A small timpani: *A 20 to 24 inch bowl.*
piede	Foot, foot pedal

pietra sonora	Resonating stones: *See "lastra di sasso" on page 144.*
piòggia di effetto	Rain machine: *See "effètto di piòggia" on page 141.*
pistolettata	Pistol shot
pollice	Thumb
pugno	Fist

R

raganèlla	Ratchet
raspa	Rasp, scraper: *A wooden or metal gourd with a serrated edge that is scraped with a thin stick. Same as a "guiro."*
raspo di metallo	A metal rasp or scraper
raspare	To scrape
reggipiato	Cymbal stand
reggitamburo	Drum stand
reso-reso	Wooden scraper: *For a guiro.*
ribeta	Jew's harp, jaw harp: *A thin metal strip attached to a frame. It is held between the teeth while plucking the metal strip. The mouth acts as a resonator.*
richiamo de (per) uccelli	Bird call or bird whistle
ricopèrta in pèlle	Leather-covered mallet
ricoperto	Muffled or muted: *"Snares off" for the snare drum.*

rivoltèlla; *rivoltèllata;* *rivoltèlla, colpi di*	Revolver, pistol shot
rombo sonore	Friction drum: *Also called a "lion's roar."*
ruggito di leone	Lion's roar
rullare	To roll: *As in a "drum roll."*
rullo	Drum roll

S

sapo Cuban	A small bamboo scraper
sassi	Stones, pebbles, rocks
sbattere	To bang
scacciapensièri	Jew's harp, jaw harp: *See "ribeta."*
scampanellio di gregge	Cowbell
scopèrto	Uncovered: *To remove a mute. Also "snares on."*
scopettine	Wire brushes
scuòtere	To shake
sega; sega cantante	Musical saw
sènza	Without
sènza còrda	Without snares
sènza sordino	Without mute
sfregare	To rub
sguilla	Cowbell

149

silofone(o)	Xylophone: *See "xilofono" on page 156.*
silofono a tastiera	Keyboard xylophone
silofono basso	Bass xylophone
silomarimba	Xylomarimba: *The full range of a xylophone and four-octave marimba.*
sinestra	Left (hand)
sirena	Siren
sirena a fiato	Mouth siren
sirena a mano	Siren operated by hand
sirena basso	Fog horn
sirena battèllo	Boat whistle
sistra(o)	Sistrum: *A metal rattle or shaker.*
sòffice	Soft
sonagli; sonaglieri	Sleigh bells
sonagli a mano	Hand bells
sonaglio	Small temple bell
sordina(o)	Mute, muffler
spazzola	Wire brushes
speròni; spròni	Spurs: *Small metal discs mounted on a handle and shaken.*
spugna	Sponge
stappare la bottiglia	Pop gun
sticcada; sticcato	Xylophone: *See "xilofono."*

strisciando; strisciato	To rub or stroke: *As in a cymbal swish. See "zischend" on page 209.*
strumenti a percussione a tastiera	Keyboard percussion instruments
sughero	Cork
sul bordo	At the edge, at the rim
sulla cassa	On the shell
sulla corda	Snares on
sulla cupola	On the dome or bell of a cymbal
sulla membrane	On the drum head
suono di bottiglia	Tuned bottles
suono di osso	Bones

T

taballi	Timpani
tabella	Slapstick
tabor	A small one or two-headed drum: *See page 176.*
taletta	Bones
tamburelli; tamburello	Tambourine
tamburello basco	Tambourine
tamburino sènza cimbali	Tambourine without jingles: *A frame drum.*

tamburo	Drum, snare drum
tamburo a calice	A goblet-shaped ceramic hand drum attached by ropes to a metal hoop
tamburo acuto	Small, high pitched snare drum
tamburo arabo	A goblet-shaped clay or metal hand drum: *Also known as a "Darabukka" or "Arabian hand drum." See page 185.*
tamburo basco	Tambourine
tamburo basso	A long drum with or without snares: *Similar to the "tambourin de provençal" in French. See page 177.*
tamburo chiaro	Snare drum
tamburo d'acciaio	Steel drum
tamburo di basilea	Parade drum
tamburo di freno	Brake drum
tamburo di frizione	Friction drum: *Lion's roar, quíca.*
tamburo di latta	Steel drum
tamburo di legno	Wood block, log drum
tamburo di legno a fessura	Slit drum, log drum
tamburo di legno Africano	Log drum
tamburo di legno pèlle	Wood plate drum: *A single-headed drum, using a thin piece of wood as a drum head. Also called a wood drum or wooden tom tom.*

tamburo grande; *tamburo grosso*	Bass drum
tamburo indiano	Indian drum
tamburo militaire	Military snare drum: *A large snare drum (6 inch shell) with calf heads and gut snares.*
tamburo orientale	Chinese drum: *A small two-headed drum with skin heads tacked on to a wooden shell.*
tamburo provenzale	A tenor drum with a long shell, which can be used with or without snares: *See "tambourin de provençal" on page 177.*
tamburo rullante	Tenor drum: *Usually played without snares.*
tamburo sènza corda	Snare drum without snares
tamburo sènza sonagli	Tambourine without jingles
tamburone	Bass drum
tavola da lavare	Washboard
tavola di legno	Wooden board
tavoletta; tavolette	Horse's hooves: *A coconut shell cut in two halves and struck on a hard surface.*
tavolette sibliante	Bull roarer: *A thin piece of wood attached to a string and whirled in the air.*
teschio cinese	Chinese temple blocks
timbales cubanis	Latin American timbales
timballi	Kettledrums

timballo	Kettledrum
timpanetti	Latin American timbales
timpani	Kettledrums
timpani a pedali	Pedal timpani
timpanista	Timpanist
timpano	A single kettledrum
timpano piccolo	A small timpani: *A 20 to 24 inch bowl.*
tintinnarie	Jingles
tiracorda	Strainer of the snare drum: *The on-off switch which activates the snares attached to the bottom head of a snare drum.*
tom tom à una pèlle	Single-headed tom tom
tom tom cinese	Chinese tom tom
treppiede	Triangle
triangolo	Triangle
trill colle monete	To play using two coins as beaters
trillo	To shake
tubi di bambù	Bamboo wind chimes
tubofono	A set of brass or steel tubes: *They are arranged on a padded table or suspended from a rack and struck with covered wooden mallets.*
tubolari	Tubular chimes
tubo sonoro	Tube shaker
tumba	Large conga drum
tuoni	Thunder sheet
tuono a pugno	Thunder sheet

U

uccelli	Bird whistle
unghia(e)	Fingernails
usignuolo	Nightingale bird call

V

velare	Mute, muffle
verga; verghe	Wire brushes
vetrata	Sandpaper blocks
vibrafono	Vibraphone:

Sounds as written.

vite-tirante
Strainer of the snare drum: *The on-off switch that activates the snares.*

X

xilofono	Xylophone: **Sounds one octave higher than written.**

xilofono a tastiera	Keyboard xylophone
xilofono basso	Bass xylophone
xilofono in cassetta di rizonanza	Early trough xylophone: *A set of wooden bars placed in a single row over a resonating box.*
xilomarimba	Xylomarimba: *The full range of a xylophone and four-octave marimba.*
xocalho	(*L. Amer.*) Metal tube shaker

Z

zilafono	Xylophone

Percussion Instruments and Terms

French

A

à deux, à2	When indicated on cymbal parts, this refers to two cymbals or "crash cymbals"
acier	Steel
agiter(z)	To shake (rub)
aiguille à tricoter	Knitting needle
allentare	To loosen
antiques cymbales	Antique cymbals: *Tuned metal discs chromatically mounted on a stand. The range is two octaves:*

Sounds two octaves higher than written.

appeau	Bird whistle
arrêter	To stop or muffle the sound
assourdit	Muted, dampened
au bord	At the edge or rim
au bord de la membrane	At the edge of the head

au centre	In the center
au milieu	In the middle
avec cordes	With snares
avec deux mains	With two hands
avec le bois	With a wood stick
avec le pouce	With the thumb: *Refers to a "thumb roll," when indicated for the tambourine.*
avec les cordes làches	To play the snare drum with snares off
avec les doigts	With fingers
avec les mains	With the hands
avec sourdine	With a mute, dampened
avec timbres	With snares: *This refers to the snares attached to the bottom head of a snare drum.*

B

baguette	Drum stick
baguette d'acier	Metal beater: *Triangle beater.*
baguette de bois	Wood stick: *Either a snare drum stick or the wood end of a timpani mallet.*
baguette d'eponge	Sponge-headed mallet: *An actual sponge head is rarely used. This term generally refers to a "soft mallet."*
baguette de metal	Metal beater: *Triangle beater.*
baguette de tambour	Snare drum sticks

baguette de timbales	Timpani mallets
baguette de timbales douce	Soft timpani mallets
baguette de timbales en bois	Wood timpani mallets
baguette de triangle	Metal triangle beater
baguette douce	Soft mallets
baguette dur	Hard mallets
baguette en cuir	Leather-covered mallets
baguette en fer	Metal beaters
baguette en jonc	Cane or rattan sticks
baguette en rotin	With the rattan end of the mallets
baguette entrechouquée	Concussion sticks: *Two short sticks made from hard wood and struck together.*
baguette mince	Thin drum sticks
baguette normale	Normal mallets
baguette ordinaire	Ordinary mallets
baguette seules	Only one stick
baguettes de bois suspendues	Wooden (bamboo) wind chimes
baguettes de verre spendues	Glass wind chimes

baguettes métalliques suspendues	Metal wind chimes
balai de jazz	Wire brushes
balais; balais métalloqie	Wire brushes
balancement	Wavy, swaying movement
bambou	Bamboo
bambou Brésilien	Brazilian bamboo shaker
bambou suspendu	Bamboo wind chimes
baril de bois	Wooden barrel or drum: *Also called a "barrel drum." A two-headed drum where the center of the shell is larger than the ends. It is played with the hands in a horizontal position, producing two different tones.*
baril de saké	Sake barrel: *A wooden barrel woven from natural fibers and played with round wooden sticks.*
basse de flandres	Bumbass: *A long pole containing two small cymbals, sleigh bells, and a small drum. A small beater strikes the drum as a wire is plucked. The cymbal and jingles are activated when the pole is struck against the floor.*
bâton	Drum stick: *Also a conductor's baton.*
batte	Stick, mallet

batterie	Percussion
battre	To beat or strike
béffroi	Alarm bell
bloc chinois	Chinese temple blocks
bloc de bois cylindrique	Cylindrical wood block: *A two-toned tubular block with open slits at both ends.*
bloc de metal; bloc métallique	Anvil, cowbell, bell plate
blocs de papier de verre	Sandpaper blocks
bloc en bois	Wood block
bois	Wood
boîte en bois	Wood block
boîto à clous	Maracas
bord	Edge, rim
bourdon	Rattle, shaker
bouteillophone	Tuned bottles
brosse	Wire brushes
bruit de sonnailles de troupeaux	Cowbell
bruit de tôle	Foil rattle

C

cadre du tambour	Drum shell
caisse	Drum

caisse à timbre	Snare drum
caisse claire	Snare drum
caisse claire grande taille	Large snare drum
caisse claire petite taille	Small snare drum
caisse plate(o)	Piccolo (small) snare drum
caisse roulante	Tenor drum: *A large drum played without snares.*
caisse roulante avec cordes	Field or parade drum with snares "on"
caisse sourde	Tom tom
calebasse	Cabasa
campanelle basse	Low-pitched bells
canard	Duck call
canne	Cane, rattan
canon	Gun, cannon shot
caoutchouc	Rubber
capoc	Mallet with a hard fiber head
carillon	A set of large tuned bells played by a manual or electronic keyboard: *Chimes can be used as a substitute.*
castagnettes	Castanets
castagnettes à manche	Handle castanets
castagnettes de fer (métal)	Metal castanets: *Mounted finger cymbals can also be used.*

castagnettes sur socle	Castanet machine
cercle	Counter hoop, rim
cercle intérieur	Flesh hoop: *The hoop attached to a drum head.*
changez, en	Change to: *An indication for the timpanist to change pitch.*
chapeau chinois	Bell tree
charleston	Hi-hat cymbals
chauffez	Excited, animated
claquebois	Xylophone
claquette; cliquette	Slapstick
cloche(s)	Chimes, large bell
cloche à (de) vache	Cowbell
cloche en lame de metal	Metal plate, bell plate
cloches plaque	Bell plate
cloches tubulaires	Chimes
clochette	Small bell
clochettes	Orchestra bells
clochettes à mains	Hand bells
cloutée	Sizzle cymbal
coque de noix	Coconut shells: *Used for making the sound of horse's hooves.*

coquilles de noix de cocs	Coconut shells
cor d'auto	Automobile horn: *See "clacson" on page 140.*
corde de boyaux	Cat gut, gut snares
cordes	Snares: *The wire or gut snares attached to the bottom head of a snare drum.*
coucou	Cuckoo bird call
coup	Drum stroke
coup de bouchon	Pop gun
coup de marteau	Hammer stroke
coup de pistolet	Pistol shot
coupes de verre	Tuned glasses
couvert	Muted, dampened
crécelle	Ratchet
crotales antiques	Antique cymbals: *See "antiques cymbales" on page 157.*
crystallophone	Tuned glasses
cuir	Leather
cuivré	Brassy tone
cymbale	Cymbal: *See "piatti" on page 147.*
cymbale chinois	Chinese cymbal
cymbale fixée à la grosse caisse	Cymbal attached to the bass drum shell
cymbale libre	Suspended cymbal
cymbale suspendue	Suspended cymbal

cymbales à doights	Finger cymbals
cymbales à l'ordinaire	Crash cymbals
cymbales à2	Crash cymbals
cymbales antiques	Antique cymbals: *See "antiques cymbales" on page 157.*
cymbales charleston à pédale	Hi-hat cymbals
cymbales digitales	Finger cymbals
cymbalier	Cymbal player

D

d'acier	Steel
décovert	Open, not muted or dampened
darboukka; derbuka	Arabian hand drum: *A single-headed, goblet-shaped hand drum made out of clay or metal with a skin head and tightened by rope or tension rods. It originates from the Middle East and North Africa and is played by holding it under the arm and striking it with fingers and hands.*
détendre	To loosen the heads of drums
détimbré	Snares off
deux plateaux	Crash cymbals

diable de bois	Pasteboard rattle: *A metal or wood shell with a single head. A gut string attached to a hole in the center of the head is vibrated against a grooved piece of wood.*
djembe	A goblet shaped hand drum
doigt	Finger
douce; doux	Soft
droite	Right: *As in "right hand."*
dur(e)	Hard

E

échelette	Xylophone:

Sounds one octave higher than written.

enclume	Anvil
éoliphone	Wind machine
épaisse	Thick
éperons	Spurs: *Small metal discs mounted on a handle and shaken.*
éponge	Sponge
étouffe(z)	Muted, dampened

F

feltro	Felt
fer	Iron, metal
feutre	Felt
fil(o)	Thread, yarn
fixée	Attached
fouet	Slapstick, whip
frappe(z)	To strike, hit
frôler	To graze or brush against
frotter; frottées	To rub or strike together
fût	Drum shell, timpani bowl

G

genou	Knee: *Using the knee and fist for playing rapid rhythms on tambourine.*
glissando avec le lever	Timpani glissando
glissando avec pédale	Timpani glissando
glockenspiel à clavier	Keyboard orchestra bells: *See "jeu de timbres" on page 169.*
gomme	Gum, rubber
gong à mamelon	Button gong
grand(e)	Large, big

grand tambour	Deep snare drum, tenor drum
grande cloche	Large church bell
grave	Low pitch
grelots	Sleigh bells
grelots de vaches	Cowbell
grosse caisse	Bass drum
grosse caisse avec pedale	Bass drum with a foot pedal
guimbarde	Jew's harp, jaw harp: *A thin metal strip attached to a frame. It is held between the teeth while plucking the metal strip. The mouth acts as a resonator.*

H

harmonica de bois	Xylophone
haut	High pitch
hochette; hochet	Baby rattle
hyoshigi	(*Jap.*) Concussion blocks: *Two short blocks of hard wood that are struck together.*

I

instruments à percussion avec clavier	Keyboard percussion instruments

J

jante, à la jante	On the rim
jazzo flute	Slide whistle
jeu à tubes	Tubular bells, chimes
jeu chromatique de cencerros	Chromatically-tuned cowbells
jeu de bouteilles	Tuned bottles
jeu de cloche	Tubular bells, chimes
jeu de clochettes	Orchestra bells
jeu de timbres	Keyboard orchestra bells: *This instrument is rarely used in orchestral music. Instead, these parts are played on orchestra bells.*
jeux de cencerros	Tuned cowbells: *These are larger and rounder than Latin cowbells. They are tuned and mounted chromatically on racks.*
jonc	Cane, rattan

L

laine	Wool
laissez vibrer	(L.V.) Let vibrate
lame d'un canif	Knife blade
lame musicale	Musical saw
libres cymbale	Suspended cymbal
liège	Cork

M

machine à écrire	Typewriter
machine à tonnerre	Thunder sheet
machine à vent	Wind machine
mâchoire	Jawbone of an ass: *The lower jawbone of a mule or donkey. When struck, the teeth rattle. The Spanish name is "quijada" and the modern version is called a "vibraslap."*
maillet	Mallet
main	Hand
mamelon	Nipple gong, button gong
manche	Handle
manche en jonc	Cane or rattan end of a mallet
maraca de métal	Metal maraca
marimbaphone	Marimba

martélement	Hammering
milieu	Middle
moteur	Motor
moyen	Middle, medium

N

noix de coco	Maracas

P

paire	Pair
paire de cymbales	Crash cymbals
pandéréta brésilienne	Jingle stick
pas de cheval	Horse's hooves
pavillon chinois	Jiggling Johnny: *A tall pole with attached jingles. When struck on the floor, the jingles are activated.*
peau	Skin drum head
peau de batterie	Batter head: *Top head of a drum.*
peau de tambour	Drum head
peau de timbre	Snare head: *Bottom head of a drum.*
peau naturale	Skin drum head
peau supérieure	Batter head of a drum

pédale de la grosse caisse	Bass drum pedal
petit(e)	Small, little
petite caisse claire	Piccolo snare drum
petite timbale	Piccolo timpani
petit tambour	Piccolo (small) snare drum
phonolithes	Stones: *A keyboard instrument made from stone disks.*
pied	Foot, with foot pedal
pierres	Stones
planche de bois	Wooden plank
planchette ronflante	Bull roarer: *A thin piece of wood attached to a string and whirled in the air.*
plaque de métal	Bell plate
plaque de tonnerre	Thunder sheet
plateaux	Crash cymbals
poing	Fist
pontet	Snare drum strainer: *The on-off switch which activates the snares attached to the bottom head of the snare drum.*
pouce	Thumb
près du bord	Near the edge or rim
prisme de pluie	Rain machine
protubérance du milieu	Dome, bell, or cup of a cymbal

Q

queue	Butt end of a drum stick
quyada	Jawbone of an ass: *The lower jawbone of a mule or donkey. When struck, the teeth rattle. The Spanish name is "quijada" and the modern version is called a "vibraslap."*

R

racler	To scrape
racleur	Rasp, scraper
rail d'acier	Steel rail or bar: *The top and side ends of the rail provide high and low-pitched sounds used for "anvil" parts.*
râpe	Rasp, guiro
râpe de bois	Wooden guiro (gourd)
râpe de metal	Metal scraper
râper	To scrape
rebord	Edge or rim
rebube	Jew's harp, jaw harp: *See "guimbarde" on page 168.*
régale de bois	Xylophone
résonateur	Resonators
rhombe	Lion's roar, bull roarer
roué à clochettes	Bell wheel: *A set of small bells attached to a revolving wheel.*

roué de la loterie	Lottery wheel: *Usually substituted with a "ratchet."*
roulante	Rolling
roulement	A "drum" roll
roulez	To roll
rugissement de lion	Lion's roar
rythmé	The pulse, beat, or time in music

S

sablier	Sandbox: *A tin cylinder filled with sand.*
sans	Without
sans cordes	Snares off
sans sourdine	Without mute
sans timbres	Snares off
sans tintements	Without jingles
scandé	Strong pulse on the units of rhythm and meter
scie musicale	Musical saw
secouer	To shake
sifflet à coulisse	Slide whistle
sifflet à roulette	Police whistle
sifflet d'oiseau	Bird whistle
sifflet du coucou	Cuckoo bird call
sifflet imité du rossignol	Nightingale bird call

sifflet signal	Boat or train whistle: *This whistle can have two or three tones.*
sifflet sirène	Mouth siren
sirène	Siren
sirène à bouche	Mouth siren
sirène aigue	High-pitched police siren
sirène grave	Low-pitched siren
sistre	Sistrum: *A metal rattle.*
sonnaile	Cowbell
sonnailles de troupeau	Alpine herd bells
sonnette	Hand bells
sonnette de table	Dinner bell
sons voiler	Muted, dampened
sourdine	Mute
sourdine interne	Internal muffler
sur la caisse	On the drum shell
sur la peau	On the drum head
sur la protubérance	On the dome, bell, or cup of a cymbal
sur le bois	On the wood
sur le bord	At the edge
sur le rebord	At (on) the rim
sur les timbres	Snares on
suspendu	Suspended

T

tablettes	Bones
tabor	A small, one or two-headed hand drum from medieval times: *This drum may be used with or without a single snare attached to one of the heads. For orchestral use, I suggest using a tom tom.*
tambour	Snare drum
tambour à corde	String drum, lion's roar
tambour à fente	Slit drum, two-tone log drum
tambour à friction	Friction drum: *The "cuíca" is a small, one-headed drum with a thin wood stick attached through the center of the head. A small piece of canvas is used to rub the stick and produce the sound. The lion's roar is a larger version of a friction drum.*
tambour arabe	Darabucca or Arabian hand drum: *See page 165.*
tambour à une seule peau	A single-headed drum
tambour avec timbres	Snare drum with snares on
tambour bongo	Bongo drums
tambour d'acier	Steel drum
tambour de basque	Tambourine

tambour de bois (Africain)	Slit drum: *A two-toned log drum.*
tambour d'empreur	Parade drum
tambour de frein	Brake drum
tambour en peau de bois	A single-headed drum with a thin sheet of wood as a drum head
tambour indien	American Indian drum
tambour militaire	A large military snare drum: *Preferably with calf heads and gut snares.*
tambour, petit	Piccolo (small) snare drum
tambour provençal	Large, narrow tenor drum: *See "tambourin de provençal" below.*
tambour roulant	Tenor drum: *Played without snares.*
tambour sur cadre	Frame drum: *A single-headed drum with no jingles.*
tambour tubulaire	Barrel drum: *A large two-headed drum played horizontally with fingers and hands. Each head produces a different tone.*
tambourin à main	Hand drum
tambourin de provençal	Tenor drum: *The largest of the tenor drums. A long, narrow shell with one or two gut snares attached to the bottom head — may be played with or without snares.*
tampon	Double-headed beater
tarole; tarolle	Piccolo (small) snare drum
timbales	Kettledrums (timpani)

timbales cubaines	Timbales
timbales orientales	Tabla drums
timpanetto	Drum with one head
tintements	Jingles
tocsin	Alarm bell
tôle	Thunder sheet
tôle à imiter le tonnerre	Thunder sheet
tom tom aigu	High-pitched tom tom
tom tom chinois	Chinese tom tom
tom tom grave	Low-pitched tom tom
tonnant	Bass drum
tonnerre à poignée	Thunder sheet
trepei	Triangle
triller avec des pieces de monnaie	Roll with coins
trolées	Roll
trompe d'auto	Taxi horn: *See "clacson" on page 140.*
trompe de brume	Fog horn
tronc d'arbre	Two-toned log drum
tubes de bambou	Bamboo wind chime
tubes de cloches	Chimes
tuyau de fer	Iron pipe

V

verge	Brushes
verres harmonica	Glass harmonica: *Glasses or bowls tuned to different pitches by adding water. They are played by rotating a finger around the rim of the glasses. Also called a "glass harp."*
verrillon	Tuned glasses
voile; voilée	Muted, dampened

X

xylophone à cassette résonant	Early trough xylophone: *A set of wooden bars placed in a single row over a resonating box.*
xylophone à clavier	Keyboard xylophone
xylophone grave	Bass xylophone

Percussion Instruments and Terms

German

A

abdämpfen	Muted, dampened
Aeoliphon	Wind machine
Afrikanische Schlitztrommel	Two-toned log drum
Alarmglocke	Alarm bell
Almglocken	Alpine herd bells: *Larger and rounder than the Latin cowbell, they are tuned chromatically and mounted on racks.*
Ambose; Amboss(β)	Anvil
am Rand	At the edge, at the rim
am Rande der Membrane	At the edge of the drum head
am Rande des Felles	At the edge of the drum head
angebunden	Attached, fixed
anschlagen	To strike, to beat
Anschlagstellen	Beating spot

antik Cymbeln; *antike Zimbeln*	Antique cymbals: *Tuned metal discs mounted chromatically on a stand with a two-octave range:*

Sounds two octaves higher than written.

Arabische *Trommel*	Arabian hand drum: *See "Darabukka" on page 185.*
Ärophon	Wind machine
auf beiden *Fellen*	On both heads
Aufbrem- *strommeln*	Brake drum
auf dem Fell	On the head
auf dem Rand	On the rim
auf dem Reifen	On the hoop
auf dem Saiten	Snares on
auf der Kuppel	On the cup, dome, bell of a cymbal
auf der Mitte	At the middle, at the center
aufgehängt	Suspended, hanging
Autohupe	Taxi horns: *See "clacson" on page 140.*

B

Bambus	Bamboo
Bambusraspel	Bamboo scraper

Bambusrohre	Bamboo wind chimes
Bambustrommel	Two chromatic octaves of small, single-headed drums mounted over resonators
Baskettrommel	Tambourine
Baskische Trommel	Tambourine
Basler Trommel	Parade drum
basque Trommel	Tambourine
bass Trommel	Bass drum
Bassxylophon	Bass xylophone
Bechertrommel	Goblet-shaped hand drum
Becken	Cymbals: *The generic term for cymbals that does not specify whether to use a suspended cymbal or a pair of crash cymbals.*
Becken auf Ständer	Suspended cymbal
Becken frei	Suspended cymbal
Becken hängend	Suspended cymbal
Beckenmaschine	Hi-hat cymbals
Becken mit Fussmaschine	Hi-hat cymbals
Becken mit Teller(n)	Crash cymbals
Becken naturlich	Crash cymbals
Becken paarweise	Crash cymbals

Beckenschlag	Cymbal crash
Becken Tambourin	Tambourine
Beckentrommel	Tambourine without a head
bedeckt	Muted, dampened: *When used for snare drum parts, it may also mean "snares off."*
befestigt	Attached, fixed
Beinklapper	Bones
belegt	To mute or dampen
Besen	Wire brushes
Blechtrommel	Steel drum
Bongo-Trommel	Bongo drums
Bremstrommeln von Autos	Brake drums
Brettchenklapper	Slapstick
Brummeisen	Jew's harp, jaw harp: *A thin metal strip attached to a frame. It is held between the teeth while plucking the metal strip. The mouth acts as a resonator.*
Brummtopf	Friction drum: *The "cuíca" is a small, one-headed version of a friction drum with a thin wooden stick attached through the center of the head. A small piece of canvas is used to rub the stick and produce the sound. The lion's roar is a larger version of a friction drum.*
Buckelgong	Button gong, nipple gong

C

Calypostrommel	Steel drum
Charleston-maschine	Hi-hat cymbals
Chinesische-becken	Chinese cymbal
Chinesische blocke	Chinese temple blocks
Chinesische tom tom	Chinese tom tom
Chinesische zimbel	Chinese cymbal
Chocolo	Metal tube shaker
Conga Trommel	Conga drum

D

dämpfen	Muted, dampened: *May also mean "snares off" when used on snare drum parts.*
Dämpfer	Mute

Darabukka; *Derbuk*	Arabian Hand Drum: *A single-headed, goblet-shaped hand drum made out of clay or metal with a skin head and tightened by rope or tension rods. It originates from the Middle East and North Africa and is played by holding it under the arm and striking it with fingers and hands.*
Darmsaite	Cat gut, gut snares
Daumen	Thumb
Donnerblech; *Donnermachine*	Thunder sheet
Doppelkonus- *trommel*	Double conical drum: *Also called a "barrel drum." The center of the shell is larger than the ends. It is played in a horizontal position with the hands, producing two different tones.*
Doppelschlag	Double-headed beater
Drahtbürste	Wire brushes
dreifacher *Vorschlag*	Drag, ruff
dumpf	Muted, dampened

E

Effektinstrumente	Sound effects
einfacher *Vorschlag*	Flam
einfellige grosse *Trommel*	Gong bass drum: *A single-headed bass drum.*

185

Einfelltrommel	Single-headed drum
Eisen	Iron
Eisenröhre	Iron pipe
Eisenschlägel	Metal beater: *Triangle beater.*
Elefantenglocken	Elephant bells: *Round brass bells from India with claw-like prongs. When shaken, an internal clapper activates the bell. Also known as "sarna bells."*
Entenquak	Duck call

F

Faßtrommel	Barrel drum: *A two-headed hand drum where the center of the shell is larger than the ends. It is played in a horizontal position with the hands and produces two different tones.*
Faust	Fist
Fell	Drum head, skin head
Filtzschlagel	Felt-headed mallet
Fingerbecken	Finger cymbals
Fingercymbeln	Finger cymbals
Fingerzimbeln	Finger cymbals
Flaschen-korkkenknall	Pop gun
Flaschenspiel	Tuned bottles

Flexaton	Flexatone: *A thin strip of steel attached to a handle with two hard beaters. The player gently shakes the handle, allowing the two beaters to strike the surface of the metal strip. The pitch can be raised or lowered by bending the strip with pressure from the thumb.*
frei Becken	Suspended cymbal
Freihängen	Suspended cymbal
Fußbecken	Hi-hat cymbals
Fußmaschine	Bass drum pedal
Fußstimm-vorrichtung	Pedal timpani

G

Gabelbecken	Metal castanets
Garn	Yarn, thread
Garnschlegel	Yarn mallet
Gebetsglocke	Temple bell
gedämpft	Muted, dampened: *May also mean "snares off" when used for snare drum.*
Gefäßrassell	Maracas
Gegenschlag-blöcke	Concussion blocks: *Two short blocks of hard wood that are struck together.*
Gegenschlag-stäben	Claves

geläute	The ringing sounds of church bells, cowbells: *Bells activated by an internal clapper.*
geschlagen	Struck
gestrichen	Stroked, rubbed
geteilt	To divide the parts: *Same as "divisi."*
gewirbelt	Rolled
gewöhnlich	Original, ordinary
Glasharmonika; Gläser	Glass harmonica: *Glasses or bowls tuned to different pitches by adding water and played by rotating a finger around the rim. Also called a "glass harp."*
Glaspapier	Sandpaper blocks
Glasstäbchen	Glass wind chimes
Gleich abdämpfen	Quickly dampen (muffle)
Gleichgriff	Matched grip
Glöckchen	Chimes: *See "Glocken" below.*
Glocke	Large bell
Glocken	Chimes:

Sounds as written.

glockenartig	Bell like
Glockenplatten	Bell plates

Glockenspiel	Orchestra bells:

Sounds two octaves higher than written.

Glockenspiel à Klavier	Keyboard orchestra bells
Glockenspiel mit Tasten	Keyboard orchestra bells
Gongstrommel	Steel drum
Griffklapper	Slapstick
grosse; große	Large, big
grosse Trommel	Bass drum
grosse trommelschlägel	Large bass drum beater
grosse Trommelstock	Large bass drum beater
Gummi	Gum, rubber

H

Halbmond	Turkish crescent, also called a "Jiggling Johnny:" *A tall pole with attached jingles. When struck on the floor, the jingles are activated.*
Hammerschalg	Hammer stroke
Handglocke	Hand bells

189

Handglockenspiel	Hand bells
Handratsche	Ratchet
Handtrommel	Tambourine
Hanfschlegel	Yarn mallet
Hängebecken	Suspended cymbal
hängend	Suspended
hängende Bambusrohre	Suspended bamboo wind chimes
hängende Becken	Suspended cymbals
hängende Glasplattchen	Suspended glass wind chimes
hart	Hard
Hartgummi-schlagel	Hard rubber mallet
Herdengeläute	Cowbells
Hi-hat Becken	Hi-hat cymbals
Hi-hat Maschine	Hi-hat cymbals
hoch	High pitch
Holz	Wood
Holzblock; Holzblock-trommel	Woodblock
Holzfass	Barrel drum: *See "Fasstrommel" on page 186.*
Holz geschlagen	To strike the wood shell of a drum
Holzhammer	Wood beater
Holzharmonika	Xylophone: *See "Xylophon" on page 209.*

Holzklapper	Slapstick
Holzplatten-trommel	Wood-plate drum: *A single-headed drum with a thin piece of wood used as a drum head.*
Holzschlägel	Wood stick, snare drum stick
Holzschlitz-trommel	Two-tone log drum, slit drum
Holzstäbe	Claves
Holzstabspiel	Xylophone: *See "Xylophon" on page 209.*
holz Tom tom	Barrel drum: *See "Fasstrommel" on page 186.*
Holzton	Wood block
Holztrommel	Wood-plate drum: *See "Holzplattentrommel" above.*
Holzraspel	Thin wood stick used as a scraper for the guiro
Holz und Schlag-instrument	Xylophone: *See "Xylophon" on page 209.*
Holz und Strohinstrument	Xylophone: *See "Xylophon" on page 209.*
Holzwindglocken	Bamboo wind chimes
Hufgtrappel	Horse's hooves
Hupe	Taxi horns: *See "clacson" on page 140.*

I

in der Mitte	In the middle
indianischer Trommel	American Indian drum
indische Schellenband	Ankle bells

J

Japanische Tempelglocken	Japanese temple bell
Javanisher Buckelgong	Javanese button (nipple) gong
Jazzbatterie	Drumset
Jazzbesen	Wire brushes

K

Kanon(e)	Cannon (shot)
Kastagnetten	Castanets
Kegeltrommel	Conical-shaped hand drum
Kessel	Kettledrum bowl
Keiselsteine	Stones: *See "Lithophon" on page 195.*
Kelchgläser	Cup-shaped glasses

Kempulgong	Gong, tam tam
Kesselpauke	Kettledrums, timpani
Kesseltrommel	Kettledrums, timpani
Ketten	Iron chains
Kinderspielzeug-trommel	Toy drum
Kirchenglocken	Church bells
Klanghölzer	Claves
Klangstäbe	Claves
Klapper; Klappholz	Slapstick
Klaviatur-glockenspiel	Keyboard orchestra bells
Klaviatur-xylophon	Keyboard xylophone
Klaxon	Hand-operated auto horn
klein(e)	Small
kleine Pauke	Piccolo timpani
kleine Trommel	Snare drum
kleine Trommel Stocken	Snare drum sticks
Klingen lassen	Let vibrate
Klingstein	Stone disks: *See "Lithophon" on page 195.*
Klöppel	Bell clapper
Klöpper	Drum sticks
Knarre	Ratchet

Knöchels	Knuckles
Knochenklapper	Bones
Kokosnußschalen	Coconut shells: *Used to make the sound of horse's hooves.*
Konustrommel	Conical-shaped hand drum
Konzertrommel	Concert snare drum
Kopf	Drum head
Kork	Cork
Kreuzschlag	Cross sticking or rim shot
Krotalen(on)	Antique cymbals: *See "antik Cymbeln" on page 181.*
Krystallophon	Glass harmonica: *See "Glasharmonika" on page 188.*
Kuba-pauken	Timbales
Kuckkuckspfeife	Cuckoo bird whistle
Kuckuck instrument	Cuckoo bird call
Kuckucksruf	Cuckoo bird call
Kuhglocke	Cowbell
Kuhglocke ohne Klöppel	Cowbell without clapper
Kuhschelle	Cowbell
Kuppel	Bell, dome, cup of a cymbal
Kürbis; Kürbisrassel	Gourd, *guiro*
Kurzwirbel	Short drum roll

L

Landsknechs-trommel	Military field drum, parade drum
Latin-amerikanische Timbales	Latin Timbales
Leder	Leather
Lederschlegel	Leather beater
Lithophon	Lithophone: *A keyboard instrument made from stone disks.*
Lochsirene	Siren
lockern	To slacken or loosen
Lotosflöte	Slide whistle
Lowengebrull	String drum, lion's roar

M

Marimbaphon	Marimba
Maschinenpauke	Machine (pedal) timpani
Maultrommel	Jew's harp, jaw harp: *A thin metal strip attached to a frame. It is held between the teeth while plucking the metal strip. The mouth acts as a resonator.*
mehrere	Many, several
Messerklinge	Knife blade

Metallblock	Anvil
Metallfolie	Thunder sheet
Metall-gefässrassel	Metal maracas
Metall-kastagnetten	Metal castanets
Metallophon	An obsolete instrument replaced by a vibraphone with the motor off
Metallplatte	Anvil
Metallraspel	Metal rasp
Metallschlegel	Metal beater
Metallwindglocken	Metal wind chimes
Militärtrommel	Military snare drum
mit	With
Mitte	Middle
mittel	Medium
Muschel-windglocken	Sea-shell wind chimes

N

Nachtigallen-schall	Nightingale bird call
Naturfell	Skin drum head
Nebelhorn	Fog horn
Nietenbecken	Sizzle cymbal
nur	Only, just

O

Oberreifen	Counter hoop of a drum
Obertonkontrolle	Internal muffler
ohne	Without
ohne Saiten	Snares off
ohne Schellen	Without jingles
ohne Schnarrsaiten	Snares off
Orkesterglockenspiel	Orchestra bells

P

Paar	Pair
paarweise Becken	Crash cymbals
Pappe Rassel	Pasteboard rattle: *A metal or wood shell with a single head. A gut string attached to a hole in the center of the head is vibrated against a grooved piece of wood.*
Paradetrommel	Parade drum
Pauke(n)	Timpani
Paukenfell	Timpani head
Paukenschlägel	Timpani mallet
Paukenwirbel	Timpani roll

Pedalbecken	Hi-hat cymbals
Pedalpauke	Pedal timpani
Peitsch; *Peitschenknall*	Slapstick, whip
Pfeife	A whistle
pfeifen; pfeifig	To whistle
Pferdegetrappel	Horse's hooves
Pikkolotrommel	Piccolo snare drum
Pistolenschuß	Pistol shot
Plastikfell	Plastic drum head
Plattenglocke	Bell plate
Polizeiflöte; *Polizeipfeife*	Police whistle

R

Rahmenrassel	Frame rattle: *Similar to a tambourine.*
Rahmentrommel	Frame drum: *A single-headed drum with no jingles.*
Rand	Rim of drum or edge of a drum head
Randschlag	Rim shot: 1. *Striking the rim and head of the drum at the same time.* 2. *Laying one stick on the head and rim and striking it with the other.*
rasch abdämpfen	Dampen quickly
Raspel	Rasp, scraper
Rassel	Rattle
Rasseln	Maracas

Rasseltrommel	Rattle drum: *A small two-headed drum with two beaters attached to the frame by cord. As the drum is rotated, the beaters strike the heads.*
Ratsche	Ratchet
Rebord	Rim, or edge of a drum head
Reco-reco	Thin wooden scraper
Regenmaschine; Regenprisma	Rain machine: *A large closed tube with screen wire inside and is filled with small pebbles. When the tube is rotated, it produces the sound of rain.*
reiben	To rub
Reibtrommel	Friction drum: *See "Brummtopf" on page 183.*
Reifen	Counter hoop, rim
Reihenklapper	Bin zasara: *A series of small pieces of wood strung together and activated by a whip-like motion by handles at each end.*
Resonanzkasten-xylophone	Early trough xylophone: *See "Trogxylophon" on page 206.*
Resonanzrohr	Vibraphone resonators
Resonatoren	Resonators
Rohr	Rattan, bamboo
Röhremrassel	Tube shaker
Röhrenglocken	Chimes: *See "Glocken" on page 188.*
Röhrentrommel	Barrel drum: *See "Fasstrommel" on page 186.*
Rohrschlegel	Rattan or bamboo sticks
Rhorstäbschen	Claves

Rolliertrommel	Tenor drum: *Without snares.*
Rollschellen	Sleigh bells
Rolltrommel	Tenor drum: *Without snares.*
Rommelpot	Friction drum: *See "Brummtopf."*
Roto tom handgestimmt	Hand-tuned roto toms
Rufend	Cuckoo imitation sound
Rührtrommel	Tenor drum: *Without snares.*
Rührtrommel mit Saiten	Tenor drum with snares
Rührtrommel tief	Tenor drum with long shell: *See "tambourin de provençal" in French on page 177.*
Rumbabirne	Maracas
Rum	Claves
Rumbakugeln	Maracas
Rumbastäbe	Claves
Rute; Ruthe	Bundle of twigs: *Struck on the head or shell of a bass drum.*

S

Säge	Musical saw
Saiten	Snares: *The wires, gut, or cable attached to the bottom head of a snare drum.*
Saiten Fell	Snare head

Saitenschraube	Snare drum strainer: *The "on-off" switch that adjusts the snares attached to the bottom head of a drum.*
Sakefaß	Sake barrel: *A wooden barrel woven from natural fibers and played with round wood sticks.*
Sandblöcke	Sandpaper blocks
Sandbüchse	Maracas
Sandpapier Blocke	Sandpaper blocks
Sandrassel	Sandbox, sand rattle: *A metal shaker filled with sand.*
Sanduhrtrommel	A hand drum shaped like an hourglass, with rope tension that changes the pitch when squeezed
Schallbecken; Schellbecken	Cymbals
Schallen- glöckchen	Buddhist temple bowl: *Small metal bowls struck with a round wooden beater.*
Schallstücke	Bell
Schelle(n)	Sleigh bells
Schellenbaum; Schellenbäume; Schellenstock	Jiggling Johnny: *A tall pole with attached jingles. When struck on the floor, the jingles are activated.*
Schellenbündel; Schellengeläute	Sleigh bells: *Small bells attached to a handle or strap. They are shaken or struck in rhythm.*

Schellenrassel; *Schellenreif*	A bunch of jingles: *Can be a tambourine without a head. It is also called a "Jiggling Johnny." See Schellenbaum on page 201.*
Schellentamburin; *Schellentrommel*	Tambourine
Schiffsglocke	Ship's bell
Schirrholz	Bull roarer: *A thin piece of wood attached to a string and whirled in the air.*
Schlag	Drum stroke
Schlagbecken	Crash cymbals
Schlagbrett	Wooden board
Schlägel	Drum stick
schlagen	To strike or hit
Schlagfell	Batter head: *Top head of a snare drum.*
Schlaginstrument	Percussion instruments
Schlaginstru- *mentengruppe*	Percussion section
Schlaginstrument *mit Klaviatur*	Keyboard percussion instruments
Schlagrassel	Jawbone of an ass, vibraslap: *The lower jawbone of a mule or donkey. When struck, the teeth rattle. The Spanish name is "quijada" and the modern version is called a "vibraslap."*
Schlagstäbe	Claves
Schlagwerk	Percussion
Schlagzeug	Percussion, drums, drum set
Schlagzeuger	Drummer, percussionist

Schlagzeug-spieler	Drummer, percussionist
Schlegel	Drum stick, mallet
Schlegel-instrumente	Mallet percussion instruments
Schlittelrohr	Metal tube shaker
Schlittenglocken; Schlitten-Schellen	Sleigh bells: *See "Schellenbündel" on page 201.*
Schlitztrommel	Slit drum, two-toned log drum
Schmirgelblock	Sandpaper blocks
Schnarre	Ratchet
Schnarrsaiten	Snares: *The wire, gut, or cable snares attached to the bottom head of a snare drum.*
Schnarrtrommel	Snare drum
Schnurrassel	Strung rattle: *Various objects such as seeds, shells, etc., strung together and tied into a bundle.*
Schnur-reibtrommel	Friction drum, lion's roar
Schotenrassel	Pod rattle: *A dried-out bean pod with seeds.*
Schraper	Scraper
Schraubenpauke	Hand-tuned timpani
Schrauben-schlüssel	Tuning handle for the timpani
Schreibmaschine	Typewriter

Schüttelrohr	Metal tube shaker
Schwamm	Sponge
Schwammschlägel	Sponge-headed beater
Schwirrholz	Bull roarer: *See "Schirrholz" on page 202.*
Sehrhoch	Snare drum
shränken	To tighten, add tension
Signalpfeife	Signal whistle: *A whistle that is made from metal or wood, about 4 inches long, with one, two, or three tones.*
singende Säge	Musical saw
Sirene	Siren
Sirenenpfeife	Siren whistle, mouth siren
Spannreifen	Counter hoop
Spieler	Player
Spielsäge	Musical saw
Sporen	Spurs: *Small metal discs mounted on a handle and shaken.*
Stabglockspiel	Orchestra bells: *See "Glockenspiel."*
Stabpandereta	Jingle stick
Stabrassel	Stick rattle: *A stick with any type of object attached to it that rattles when shaken.*
Stahl	Steel
Stahlbesen	Wire brushes
Stahllöffel	Steel spoons
Stahlspiel	Orchestra bells: *See "Glockenspiel."*
Stahlstäbe	Metal claves

Stahltrommel	Steel drum
Stampfrohr; *Stampftrommel*	Stamping tube: *Tuned bamboo tubes that are activated when struck on the ground.*
Standglocke	Temple bell
Steine	Stones
Steinplatten; *Steinspeil*	Lithophone: *See "Lithophon" on page 195.*
Stempelflöte	Slide whistle
Stiel	Handle
Stielkastagnetten	Handle castanets
Stock	Stick
Stock auf Stock	Stick-on-stick, rim shot
Stricknadel	Knitting needle
Strohfiedel	Straw fiddle, xylophone: *An early xylophone with bars separated by straw.*
Strosstrommel	Stamping tube: *See "Stampfrohr" above.*
Sturmglocke	Storm bell: *Similar to "Schiffsglocke."*

T

Table Trommeln	Tabla drums
Tambourin	Tambourine
Tamburi	Timpani
Tamburin	Tambourine
Tastenxylophon	Keyboard xylophone
Teller(n)	Crash cymbals

Templeblöcke	Temple blocks
Templeglocke	Japanese temple bells
Tenortrommel	Tenor drum
Tibetanische Gebetsteine	Tibetan prayer stones
Ti(s)chglocke	Dinner bell
tiefe Glocke	Low-pitched bell
tiefes Glockengeläute	Chimes: *See "Glocken" on page 188.*
Tierschelle	Cowbell
Timbales	Latin Timbales
Tom tom spiel	Roto toms
Triangel	Triangle
Triangelschlegel	Triangle beater
Trillerpfeife	Police whistle
Trinadad Gongtrommel	Steel drum
Trogxylophon	Early trough xylophone: *A set of wooden bars placed in a single row over a resonating box.*
Trommel(n)	Drum
Trommelfell	Drum head
Trommelreifen	Counter hoop
Trommelschlegel	Drum sticks
Trommelstocken	Drum sticks
Trommelwirbel	Drum roll

Tubaphon; *Tubuscampano-* *phon*	A set of brass or steel tubes: *They are arranged on a padded table or suspended from a rack and struck with padded wood mallets.*
Tumbadora	Conga drum: *The large tumba.*
Türkische becken	Turkish cymbals
Turmglockenspiel	Chimes, carillon bells
Tympali;Tympelles	Timpani

U

umstimmen	To change or retune a pitch
Unterreifen	Flesh hoop: The hoop attached to a drum head.

V

verklingen lassen	Let vibrate
Verstärkungs- *Röhre*	Resonators
verstimmung	Out of tune
Vibraphon	Vibraphone
Vibraphon- *schlägel*	Vibraphone mallet
Vibraphonspieler	Vibraphone player
Viehschelle(n)	Cowbell
Vogelgesang	Nightingale bird call

W

Wachtel	Quail bird call
Wachtelpfeife	Quail bird whistle
Waldteufel	Friction drum: *See "Brummtopf" on page 183.*
Walxentrommel	Walzentrommel: *A very large two-headed drum from the 16th Century. It may be replaced by a military snare drum.*
Waschbrett	Washboard
wechseln	To change or retune a pitch
weich	Soft
weiche Schlägel	Soft felt mallet
weicher Filz	Soft felt
Wellensirene	Siren
Wickelreifen	Flesh hoop: *See "Unterreifen" on page 207.*
Wiege	Early trough Xylophone: *See "Trogxylophon" on page 206.*
Windglocken	Wind chimes
Windmaschine	Wind machine
Wirbel	Drum roll
Wirbeltrommel	Tenor drum
Wolle	Wool
Wollschlägel	Wool-headed mallet

X

Xylophon   Xylophone:
Sounds one octave higher than written.

Z

Zarge	Drum shell
Ziehpfeife	Slide whistle
ziemlich	Medium
Zilia	A small pair of cymbals
Zimbel(n)	Antique cymbals: *See "antik Cymbeln" on page 181.*
zischend	Swish: *A technique used for crash cymbals. The edge of one cymbal slides across the inside of the other cymbal.*
zu 2	With two players: *When used for cymbal parts, it refers to crash cymbals.*
zurückstimmen	To change or retune a pitch
zusammen-schlagen	To crash two cymbals together
Zweifelltrommel	Two-headed drum
Zylindertrommel	Cylinder drum

String Terms and Directives

Italian

abbassare   A request made by composers to purposely retune a string of a violin, etc. for a special effect: *See "heraustimmen" on page 229.*

anima   The "soul" or sound post of a string instrument

a punta(o) d'arco   With the point (tip) of the bow:

Symphonie Fantastique - Hector Berlioz

arco in giù   Down bow :

arco in su   Up bow:

bariolage	A rapid alternation between two or more strings in one bow or separate bows
cantino	The highest string on a violin
colofonia	Resin
corda	String section
corda vuota	Composers indicate the use of "open strings" by adding a circle (O) over the note:

Hoe-Down from Rodeo - Aaron Copland

cordiera	Tail piece of a string instrument
divisi	Two lines of music or double stops that are intended to be played by two separate players:

The Three-Cornered Hat - Manuel de Falla

divisi, non

When parts are written to be played as "double stops:"

Capriccio Espagnol - Nikolay Rimsky-Korsakov
II Variazoni

flautando

A flute-like tone: *Produced by tilting the bow so as to use less hair. Played near the fingerboard.*

Music for String Instruments Percussion and Celesta - Béla Bartók

legno, col

With the wood of the bow:

Symphonie Fantastique - Hector Berlioz
Witches' Sabbath

| **martellato** | Short, sharp, detached strokes: *Without lifting the bow off the strings.* |

Das Klagende Lied - Gustav Mahler

| **ossia** | Or: *An alternative to the written part.* |

Sonata - Serge Prokofieff
2. Scherzo

| **pizzicato** | (*pizz.*) Plucking the strings, usually with the forefinger: *The following is an unusual example that uses the thumb and forefinger.* |

Three Pieces from "Romeo and Juliet" Ballet - Serge Prokofieff

| **ponticèllo** | The bridge of a string instrument |

ponticèllo, sul   Play near the bridge:

Scheherazade - N. Rimsky-Korsakov
IV

portamento   Sliding from one note to another:
Sounding all the pitches in between.

Daphnis and Chloe - Maurice Ravel

portato   Well articulated: *Sometimes thought of as
"half staccato" and "half legato."*

punto, al   At the point (tip) of the bow:

El Salón México - Aaron Copland

Violin

quasi guitara   To strum the strings like a guitar:

Capriccio Espagnol - N. Rimsky-Korsakov
V Fandango asturiano

saltando; saltato   A general term for bowed string instruments. The bow is allowed to bounce on the string with rapid movements in one direction:

Capriccio Espagnol - N. Rimsky-Korsakov
V Fandango asturiano

scordatura   A request made by composers to purposely retune a string of a violin, etc., for a special effect: *See "heraustimmen" on page 229.*

Spalliera   Shoulder rest

spiccato	A technique for bowed string instruments by rapidly bouncing the bow on the strings: *Usually played in the central portion of the bow.*

Capriccio Espagnol - N. Rimsky-Korsakov

III Alborado

spiccato assai	Very detached and separated:

Capriccio Espagnol - N. Rimsky-Korsakov

IV Scena e canto gitano

staccato - (stac.)	Detached, separated: *Allowing space between the notes. The slur indicates this is to be played in one bow direction.*

Symphony No. 5 - Gustav Mahler

3rd Movement

strappare	To rip or tear: *A strong down-bow or pizzicato attack. See "anreissen" on page 225.*

***sulla corda* I**	To play on the G string: *The Roman numerals: I, II, III, IV determine which string to use.*
sul G (D) (A) (E)	Indicates the string on which to play the passage:

Scheherazade - N. Rimsky-Korsakov

III

tallone, al	To play at the frog or end of the bow: *Also referred to as the "nut" or "heel" of the bow.*

Manon Lescaut - Giacomo Puccini

Atto Quarto

tastiera, sulla; ** *tasto, sul***	Bowing lightly over (near) the fingerboard to produce a flute-like effect:

Pictures From An Exhibition - Modest P. Mussorgsky

3. Tuileries

unisiono	(*unis.*) To play together or revoke a direction — such as "*divisi.*"

String Terms and Directives

French

à deux corda	On two strings
âme	The "soul" or sound post of a string instrument
archet; archetto	Indicates the use of a bow
arraché	To rip, tear: *Strong down-bow or pizzicato attack.*

Concerto for Piano and Orchestra - Aaron Copland

avec le bois de l'archet	With the wood of the bow:

XII Symphonie - Darius Milhaud
(RURALE)

avec le bois de l'archet

avec le dos de l'archet	To use the back (wood) of the bow: *Similar to "col legno" in Italian.*

Rapsodie Espagnole - Maurice Ravel

baisser l'accord	A request made by composers to purposely retune a string of a violin, etc., for a special effect: *See "heraustimmen" on page 229.*
bariolage	A technique for string players where a group of notes are played without position changes on two or more strings by rapidly alternating the bow
brisé	Short, detached movements of the bow
chanterelle	The highest string of a violin
chevalet, près du	To play near the bridge of the violin:

Rondes de Printemps - Claude Debussy

colophane	Resin

corde	String or string instrument
corde à vide; *corde à jour*	Open string: *See "corda vuota" on page 211.*
cordier	Tail piece of a string instrument
coup d'archet	A stroke of the bow
cousin	Shoulder rest
dehors, en	To play outside the normal position: *Over the fingerboard.*

Daphnis and Chloe - Maurice Ravel

détaché	Separated or detached strokes:

Petrouchka - Igor Stravinsky
The Shrove - Tide Fair

flageolet	To play harmonics:

Also sprach Zarathustra - Richard Strauss

fouetté	Whipping the bow: *Accent on an up bow with energy.*

jeté   A thrown-bow technique: *Using the upper part of the bow so the bow rebounds several times with a down-bow direction.*

Histoire Du Soldat - Igor Stravinsky
The Soldier's March

louré   Slightly detached notes played on the string

martelé   Short, sharp, detached strokes: *Without lifting the bow off the strings.*

Arcana - Edgard Varèse

martelé du talon   Using the heel (frog) of the bow for the *martelé* stroke:

Symphonie - Henri Dutilleux
Finale, Con Variazioni

mettez les sourdines   To put on the mute

ôter les sourdines	To take off the mute
pincé	Pinched, *pizzicato*
piqué	Short, detached strokes: *A form of staccato that uses more of a bouncing attack. The slur indicates the notes are played in one bow direction.*

piquiren	To play *spiccato*: *See "spiccato" on page 216.*
pointe, de la	With the point (tip) of the bow:

Rondes de Printemps - Claude Debussy

poussé; poussez	Up bow:

quasi Guitara le Violon sous le bras
Strum like a guitar while holding the violin under the arm:

Iberia - Claude Debussy

Mouv de la Marche
quasi Guitara le Violon sous le bras

1ers vons

pizz. **pp**

restez
Remaining in one position while playing a passage:

Histoire Du Soldat - Igor Stravinsky
Ragtime

Vl.

restez

f

ricochet
Throwing the bow on the string either in an up or down-bow direction

sautillè
A fast *staccato* using all down bows:
The bow lightly rebounds off the string.

Arcana - Edgard Varèse

sec. sautillè

Vons

p

sur Sol   To play the passage entirely on the G string: *Also "sur Re," "sur La," and "sur Mi."*

La Valse - Maurice Ravel

talon, au (du)   To play at the heel (frog) of the bow:

The Scorcerer's Apprentice - Paul Dukas

tire(z)   Down bow:

touche, sur la   To bow over the fingerboard:

Rapsodie Espagnole - Maurice Ravel

String Terms and Directives

German

Abstreich	Down bow:

(musical notation: down bow)

anreissen	To rip, tear: *Strong down-bow or pizzicato attack. See "gerissen" page 227.*
***auf* I**	To play on the E string
***auf* II**	To play on the A string
***auf* III**	To play on the D string
***auf* IV**	To play on the G string
Aufstrich	Up bow:

(musical notation: up bow)

Bogen	The bow for string instruments
Bogenspitze, mit	With the point (tip) of the bow:

Drei Orchesterstücke - Alban Berg
III. Marsch

Bogenstreich	The bow Stroke

Bogenwechsel, viel	Many changes of the bow:

Drei Orchesterstücke - Alban Berg
II. Reigen

1^{rs} Violons

f viel Bogenwechsel

Bratschen "col legno" geschlagen	Violas
	Hit with the wood end of the bow:
	Here, the German composers borrow "col legno" from the Italian and combine it with a German verb.

Drei Orchesterstücke - Alban Berg
II. Reigen

Br.

p

col legno geschl.

Dämpfer	Mute: *mit Dämpfer (with mute). Dämpfer weg (without mute).*
Doppelgriffe dreifach	Double stop
	Play as a "triple stop:"

Also sprach Zarathustra - Richard Strauss

dreifach

Bratschen

pp

Flageolett	See "*flageolet*" in French on page 220.
Frosch	Frog: *As in "am Frosch," playing at the "frog" (nut) end of the bow.*

Don Quixote - Richard Strauss

am Frosch

Geige	Violin
gerissen (ab)	To rip or tear with a strong down-bow attack:

Symphony No. 5 - Gustav Mahler

II.

geteilt	To divide the parts; not to be played as "double stops:" *Same as "divisi" in Italian.*

Till Eulenspiegels lustige Streiche - Richard Strauss

geteilt, nicht	One player, *non divisi: Play as double stops.*

Also sprach Zarathustra - Richard Strauss

gestossen	Disconnected, *staccato:*

Till Eulenspiegels lustige Streiche - Richard Strauss

geworfen	Bouncing the bow rapidly on the strings: *Similar to "saltando" (It.).*
gezupft	To pluck a string: *Same as pizzicato.*
Glissando mit einem Finger	A written-out glissando, using one finger:

Symphony No. 2 - Gustav Mahler
3rd Movement

Glissando mit einem Finger.

Griffbrett, am (dem)

Playing with the bow over the fingerboard:

Drei Orchesterstücke - Alban Berg
I. Präludium

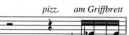

heraustimmen, gestimmt

A request made by composers to purposely retune a string of a violin, etc., for a special effect:

Symphony No. 4 - Gustav Mahler

NB. Der 1. Sologeiger hat sich mit 2 Instrumenten zu versehen, von denen eine um einen Ganzton höher, das andere normal gestimmt ist.

Herstrich

Down bow:

Hinstrich

Up bow:

Kolophonium

Resin

martellato (It.)   Corelli (or the editor) explains his use of this Italian word with the German phrase, *"at the point without leaving the string:"*

Sonata - folies d'Espagna - Arcangelo Corelli
La Foglia

martellato
an der Spitze ohne die zu verlassen

Pultweise geteilt	Divisi by stand
Saitenhalter	Tailpiece of a string instrument
Schulterstütze	Shoulder rest
Seele	The "soul" or sound post of a string instrument
Spitze	Point or tip of the bow:

Symphony No. 7 - Anton Bruckner
IV. SATZ Finale

p   Spitze

springend; spring Bogen   Bouncing the bow:

Das Klagende Lied - Gustav Mahler

Stange   The wood part of the bow: *As in "Stange geslagen" (playing on the strings with the wood part of the bow).*

Steg, am   To play near the bridge of a string instrument: *Producing a metallic sound.*

Symphonie - Anton Weber
I - Meiner Tochter Christine

Stimmstock   The "soul" or sound post of a string instrument

Streich   Stroke: *As in "breiter Strich" (broader stroke).*

Streichen   To bow

Strich für Strich Separate bows:

Das Klagende Lied - Gustav Mahler

Strich für Strich

Streicher String section
tiefer stimmen A request made by composers to purposely retune a string of a violin, etc., for a special effect: *See "heraustimmen" on page 229.*

About the Author

Anthony J. Cirone, former Percussionist with the San Francisco Symphony, performed under the musical directorship of Josef Krips, Seiji Ozawa, Edo DeWaart, Herbert Blomstedt, and Michael Tilson Thomas. He also played with noted guest conductors: Leonard Bernstein, Igor Stravinsky, Aaron Copland, Eugene Ormandy, Kurt Mazur, Rafael Kubelik, and James Levine.

Cirone was Professor of Music at San José State University where he also conducted the Percussion Ensemble and taught Manuscript Preparation/Computer Engraving. He served on the faculty at Stanford University and Chaired the Percussion Department for the Jacobs School of Music at Indiana University.

Mr. Cirone has over 100 published titles, including textbooks, symphonies for percussion, sonatas, a string quartet, and seven works for orchestra. His *Portraits in Rhythm* for snare drum is used for auditions, competitions, and training percussionists throughout the world. His latest endeavors include: *On Musical Interpretation of Percussion Performance* (a composite of his pedagogy and concertizing) and *Cirone's Pocket Dictionary of Foreign Musical Terms* (for use by composers, conductors, and performers).

Cirone won the Modern Drummer's Magazine poll for Outstanding Percussionist, five years in a row, including him in their Hall of Fame. He was also a recipient of the ASCAP Rudolf Nissim Composition Contest, winning a Special Distinction Award for his *Pentadic Striations for Orchestra*. In 2007, he received the Percussive Arts Society's distinct honor of being inducted into their Hall of Fame.

Mr. Cirone was Percussion Consultant/Editor for Belwin-Mills, Publishing Co., Warner Bros. Publishing Co., Columbia Pictures Publications, and currently is the Executive Editor of Percussion Publications for Meredith Music, a Clinician for the Avedis Zildjian Cymbal Company, the Yamaha Corporation, and Remo, Inc.